Chinese Myths and Legends

Joanne O'Brien is the author and editor, with Kwok Man Ho, of several books on Chinese arts and astrology. She has also extensively researched and written on religions both ancient and modern, as well as appearing on television and working for an international consultancy.

Kwok Man Ho is a professional geomancer and astrologer. He studied for eighteen years in the Buddhist and Taoist monasteries of Hong Kong and China.

From the same authors in Arrow
CHINESE HOROSCOPES

Chinese
Myths and Legends

JOANNE O'BRIEN

Translated and illustrated by
Kwok Man Ho

ARROW BOOKS

Arrow Books Limited
20 Vauxhall Bridge Road, London SW1V 2SA

An imprint of Random Century Group

London Melbourne Sydney Auckland
Johannesburg and agencies throughout
the world

First published in Great Britain by Arrow 1990

Photypeset by Input Typesetting Ltd, London
Printed and bound in Great Britain by
Courier International, Tiptree, Essex

ISBN 0 09 962060 X

Contents

Contents

Introduction
MARTIN PALMER

The Chinese people have one of the oldest collections of literature in the world. Their legends and myths, dating back to over two thousand years BC, have been passed down to this century through spoken and written traditions. We have access to histories, poems, prayers and stories which come from a time when the pyramids were young and Stonehenge newly begun. It should not be a surprise, therefore, to discover that Chinese literature also holds one of the world's richest stores of tales and legends. Much of the earliest literature of China is concerned with dynastic histories which consist of wonderfully told stories, etching out the beginnings of the Chinese state and people. The great religious teachers of China, especially the Taoists and Buddhists, used storytelling as one of the main ways of spreading the beliefs of their faiths. A preoccupation with ghosts, the dead and the supernatural, as well as imaginative accounts of how things came to be, has always been present in China. Even the old sceptic Confucius had to acknowledge this, although he refused

7

to comment on the supernatural, saying he had enough trouble trying to sort out this world, let alone any others!

Ancient scholarly writings and popular oral folk tales are the original source of Chinese myths and legends. The first tradition of scholarly writing arose from the demands of the Chinese examination system, which was formalized and rigid. Scholars spent twenty or more years learning the classics of Confucius off by heart. Confucius, who lived in *c.* 551–479 BC, looked back to the stories contained in the written records of the olden times. There he found what he saw as being an account of the proper way a country and its people should be ruled. From this Confucius developed his theories both of statecraft and of proper relationships within the family. This was based upon respect for one's elders, of the female for the male, of the son for the father and of the people to the Emperor. It was these values which the scholars imbibed while reading the classic texts of Confucius. They were then expected to be able to use quotations or illustrations from these texts, known as The Five Classics, to solve the day to day political, social and economic problems which, as the ruling class, they were called upon to handle. This rigid adherence to The Five Classics and the style of literature which these embodied did little for creative writing. The stories produced by writers educated under this system, which lasted over 2000 years, tend to be moralistic or exemplary tales, often taking an historical figure whose behaviour highlights a Confucian value or teaching. As such they usually lack a certain vitality which is the hallmark of the other major source of Chinese myths and legends – the folk or popular tales. Furthermore, Confucianists were not given to toying with the supernatural since they saw themselves as dealing on the whole with verifiable facts: history, geography or biography. The shady area of legend and myth was left to the other dimension of the Chinese storytelling world – the religious and folk world.

Apart from Confucianism, which is often not thought

of as a religion but more as a code by which to live and govern, there are two other belief systems or religions which have shaped Chinese society. These are Taoism and Buddhism. It is from these two faiths and the folk religion of the ordinary people which they inspired that the majority of the tales and legends in this book come.

Present-day Taoism descends from Shamanism, China's earliest religion. Shamanism, still practised to this day in parts of Japan, China and even Siberia – its original homeland – believes in two parallel worlds: our material world and a spiritual world. The spiritual world has influence on and participates in our world, but we in this world normally have no access to the spiritual world. However, through the medium of a shaman, the two worlds meet. Through trances, and through possession by the spiritual world, a shaman can communicate between both worlds. The shamanistic world view also imbues the material world with spirit forces which manifest themselves through the natural forces. Shamanism therefore sees humanity's role as that of treading a careful path, a path indicated and marked out by the spiritual world and in keeping with its expression through the natural forces and order of the world.

Taoism's roots are in Shamanism. The name Taoism is derived from the Chinese word '*Tao*' which can best be translated as meaning 'The Way' or 'The Path'. It refers to the natural, cosmic Path or Way which Heaven has ordained and which earth and humanity should follow. To fail to follow the Way brings problems and distress because one is out of step – out of harmony – with the natural way of things.

There are two main expressions of Taoism. The first form arose from the writings and teachings of the sage, Lao Tzu. Lao Tzu is supposed to have lived in the fifth century BC and to have written a book known as the *Tao Te Ching* which roughly translated means *The Book of the Way*. From this book, which posits that the wise man flows

9

with the stream, bends with the wind and thus triumphs by being a part of the natural ordering of the universe, grew a school of philosophy and a way of life. Taoist sages, living quiet lives of contemplation in the forests or on the mountains, can still be found to this day. By withdrawing from the ordered, busy world, which was controlled by state Confucianism, the sages immersed themselves in contemplation and in special exercises designed to confer not just wisdom and magical powers but even immortality. This quest for immortality still lies at the heart of much Taoist ritual and story. Taoists believe that if you become perfectly attuned to the cosmic forces of yin and yang, then you will live for ever. These strange 'men of the mountains', the Taoist adepts, are frequently found in the tales and legends of China. Alongside them are set the immortals themselves, who appear in the tales as friends of the friendless and defenders of the poor and the weak. The story of 'Five Men Mountains' captures many of these ideas.

There are few who can aspire to the state of being a sage, even fewer who can hope for immortality. And thus there arose a more popularist form of Taoism in which divine forces in the shape of gods and goddesses, magic spells, incantations and priests offered a path to, if not immortality, at least some sense of salvation and meaning in this life and the next.

It was towards the end of the second century AD that there arose leaders of popular Taoism who offered cures in the here-and-now and salvation or wellbeing in the hereafter. Chief amongst these was Chang-Tao-ling, who stands as the archetype of the Taoist priest and leader of popular Taoism. He was credited with being a magician, a healer, an exorcist and a priest. His charms are still published every year in the annual Almanac, the most popular book of the Chinese, outside mainland China. His sword, used for exorcising ghosts, hung until the 1930s in a vast temple compound where his descendants had lived from the ninth century. His magic and rituals are still in use today among Chinese communities throughout the world. Yet Chang-Tao-ling was also a rebel and founded what became, for a short time, an independent state. The story of 'The Rats' Wedding' features a descendant of Chang-Tao-ling, who was the receptacle of all the magical powers associated with Chang.

The Taoists who appear in the stories and tales in this book swing between these two extremes of the sage and the magician priest. The sage is the symbol of tranquillity and wisdom. But the Taoist priest is more complex. Sometimes he is the bringer of wisdom or the solver of problems, such as hauntings. At other times he is a charlatan and a good-for-nothing, causing trouble and deceiving the honest man. This accurately reflects the different types of priests who dwelt in traditional China.

The second of the major faiths of China is Buddhism. Buddhism did not originate in China. The Buddha lived in North India some five hundred years BC. His teachings, spread by the communities of monks which he founded, took some time to travel to China. As far as we can tell, the earliest evidence of Buddhism in China comes from around the time of Christ. By the time he had reached China, the Buddha had ceased to be a purely human figure, and was now a denizen of Heaven, with all the powers that arose from that. As a foreign religion Buddhism was not accepted by either the Confucians or the Taoists. Indeed, the Taoists felt deeply threatened by Buddhism and it is quite possible that popular Taoism arose as much as an attempt to combat Buddhism as for any other reason.

It took Buddhism many hundreds of years to establish itself in China and it was not until after the last major persecution of the faith in the ninth century that Buddhism can be said to have become an accepted part of Chinese life. One reason for this long period of assimilation was the strong Chinese dislike of the idea of celibate monks.

It was a disaster for the Chinese not to have a family because ancestor worship formed such an integral part of Chinese life. Celibacy heralded the breaking of family ties, and the absence of children was a blow at the very heart of Chinese society. This distrust of monks and lack of respect for them has continued to this day and is frequently expressed in the great novels and stories of China. The Buddhist monk may be treated with courtesy; he may be welcomed at certain times in the life of a family, but he is still often mistrusted. Furthermore, while Taoists rarely if ever went in for fasting, abstinence from sex or drink (excepting the sages, who were seen to be almost of another world), Buddhist monks had to live according to the precepts of their faith, which forbade drink, sexual intercourse and, in many cases, meat. This set them apart, and many are the stories which tell gleefully of the sexual, alcoholic or meat-eating exploits of Buddhist monks and nuns. This is reflected in the Taoist story 'The Mad Monk' in which the behaviour of the Buddhist monk is a deliberate parody of Buddhism.

In terms of the popular religion and culture of the ordinary Chinese, Buddhism's major impact came through the deities it introduced and the idea that there was a scale of meritorious actions which, if followed, could lead you to heaven or at least to a good rebirth. Of the gods and goddesses, none is more popular than the Bodhisattva Kuan Yin. The term Bodhisattva refers to someone who through countless rebirths has reached a level of such perfection and goodness that he/she does not have to be reborn again but can pass instead into ultimate freedom, the state of Nirvana. This is explained in the story 'Kuan Yin'. However, the Bodhisattvas do not pass into Nirvana. They are too concerned by the suffering of people and creatures on the earth. They can see that most people, by their own actions, are unable to aspire to goodness and thus escape the wheel of rebirth, sorrow, pain, death and rebirth. Therefore, in order to help them, the Bodhisattvas hold back from final release and, if anyone calls upon them for help, they will try to answer that call. Kuan Yin, the Mother Goddess, is the most popular for she offers help to all who ask. She is wise, kind but firm. She comes to the help of mothers and of the young, but also protects the poor and the weak.

Here perhaps is the most important key to understanding the stories in this book: the poor and the weak. The tales we give here are translations from collections of tales published for or told by the ordinary people of China. In them the weak and the poor, the helpless and the naive, are seen to triumph over the proud and the wealthy, the scholarly and the corrupt. It is the little man against the world. One of the best examples is the story 'Ma Chen and the Immortal Brush Pen' in which not only does the corrupt and vicious local official get his just reward but so does the evil Emperor. In these stories the oft oppressed peoples of China found relief and hope. Here are pictures of what the peasants and the workers hoped might happen. That it rarely ever did makes the tales even more poignant. In this category come the 'special gift' stories in which a poor or humble person receives a fabulous magical gift which transforms his or her life. That this has to be linked to purity of heart makes the contrast with the grasping officials around the protagonist even more stark. The story of 'The Dumb Flute Player' captures this perfectly.

Finally there are a few key terms which need a brief explanation. We have already mentioned yin and yang. In Chinese thought the world, indeed the entire universe, is kept in motion through the existence of yin and yang. Yin and yang are complete opposites, dark and light, female and male, cold and hot, wet and fiery, black and white, and so on. The struggle for supremacy between these two forces is what keeps the world spinning and life moving. Neither one can ever win, but their dynamic tension is what fuels the life forces of the universe. They are not gods, but the elemental forces of nature and of all existence.

Heaven is often referred to in the stories. But Heaven is not the Heaven of Christian stories. Heaven is one of the three basic groups of the universe. The other two are Earth and Humanity. Between the three are found the major expressions of yin and yang. Heaven is yang, Earth is yin and Humanity sits between them, composed of both yin and yang, of the Earth yet in touch with Heaven. In each human the forces of Heaven and Earth are to be found intermingled. It is we who help to keep the balance between the forces and powers of the universe. The Emperor of China was always referred to as the Son of Heaven. Each year he sacrificed to Heaven and Earth in order to restore the balance of the universe. And Heaven and Earth should not be seen as being gods or even God. Again, they are the natural forces, the True Way of existence. To be out of harmony with the Will of Heaven meant to run the risk of being crushed by the inevitable Way of Heaven. True, Taoism came to populate Heaven with gods and even with divine emperors. This is the origin of the Jade Emperor, ruler, albeit not always a very effective one, of the Taoist pantheon of deities in Heaven. Buddhism, too, constructed a sort of Heaven where Kuan Yin resided and kept watch upon the people of earth. Buddhism and Taoism also constructed elaborate hells containing indescribable horrors. Yet, when all is said and done, the basic Chinese triad of Heaven, Humanity and Earth, is not so much a divine idea, rather a description of the building blocks of reality.

So what of the gods and goddesses who will flit through these pages? Taoism peopled the world with deities. Every place has its earth god, its local god, its regional god. Strange rocks, gnarled old trees, meandering rivers are all full of supernatural forces. The world of the shamans is still alive and well in the world of popular Chinese belief. Nor are the gods of Taoism separated from the Bodhisattvas of Buddhism. At the popular level they are all manifestations of the divine and the supernatural. It is from this wonderfully rich, intense and highly-charged mixture that the strength, vitality and fundamental attraction of the Chinese tales and legends come.

Rice from Heaven

Long before books were written or records kept, the land of China was covered with forests and trees. There were no paddy fields, no shops, no markets and no roads. Nomads hunted in the forest for wild animals and ate fruit and berries that grew in abundance.

One late spring the monsoon rains arrived as usual, but instead of subsiding as everyone expected, the rains continued to beat down unceasingly for more than two months. The nomads sought shelter in caves near the mountains' peaks, but the forests were devastated and the animals drowned. The earth looked like a barren lake. Eventually the rains began to subside, the trees came into view and the nomads began a wary descent down the mountainsides. Slowly the animals that had sought shelter on the higher levels began to emerge. First of all, rabbits appeared, then squirrels and finally tigers, all desperate to find food in this waste land. The tigers took control of the land, hunting, killing and eating everything that came their way. The humans were forced to make forays into the forest from their caves in the mountains but with the tigers

16

roaming the land scavenging for food they no longer felt safe.

Far away, beyond the land of humans, there was an island in the Eastern Sea governed by the Jade Emperor. The gods and Immortals who lived here had watched the humans suffer untold hardships and, out of sympathy for their plight, they decided to convene an emergency council.

The Jade Emperor spoke first. 'You have seen for your-selves what has happened on the earth. Now we need to find a way to help the humans. Who has any suggestions?'

The Five Grains God rose before the assembled audi-ence. 'I have a plan I want you all to consider. Why don't we teach the people to grow and harvest rice? We have enjoyed its benefits from the moment of creation – perhaps it is their turn to taste the crop of the gods. They would no longer need to compete with the tigers for the food of the forest.'

A murmur of agreement ran through the council at this suggestion and the god Fu Hsi Shih called out loudly, 'We can do more than that. Why don't we send them assistants so their future is secured?'

Once more the gods murmured in agreement.

'Well, that's decided,' announced the Jade Emperor. 'I will appoint a horse, a cow, a sheep, a dog, a cock and a pig. The cow and the horse will help to plough, to pull the carts and harvest the rice, the sheep will produce milk, the cock will waken them each morning and the dog will guard their houses. The pig doesn't need to work – he can eat and sleep as much as he wants, but he must be willing to sacrifice himself for human food.'

Before nightfall everything was organized, but as the animals were preparing to sail across the Eastern Sea the Jade Emperor called everything to a halt.

'We've forgotten about the paddy fields. How can we transport the rice across the Eastern Sea?'

There were abundant fields of rice throughout the gods'

island and each stalk was heavily laden with grain from its root to its tip. It would be pointless to tie it in bales and float it across the Eastern Sea as it might be tossed in the wrong direction or scattered by the turbulent waves. Once again the Five Grains God came up with an answer: why not attach the rice to one of the animals?

First of all the Jade Emperor asked the cow to carry the rice. But the cow shook his head and sighed. 'I know I'm endowed with great power and have a fine physical body, but I'm not particularly skilled. I think you should ask the horse.'

But before the Emperor had a chance to say anything the horse neighed loudly in refusal. 'No, I'm a poor choice. I have such fine hair that the rice grains would slip off my sleek coat. Why don't you ask the cock?'

The Jade Emperor turned to the cock, but the cock had already prepared an excuse. 'Your Highness, look at me,' he crowed. 'I'm small and weak. I couldn't possibly bear the weight.'

By this time the sheep and the pig had also found plausible excuses not to make the delivery.

So far the dog had watched everyone without uttering a word and now he came forward to speak to the Jade Emperor. 'I know that the humans are in a desperate situation so I'm willing to carry the grain across the Eastern Sea.'

The dog was dipped in a heavenly pool and sent to the granary to roll in the rice in order to cover his body with grains. When he emerged every inch of his body except for his eyes was covered with grains of rice.

The assembled animals gathered at the shore and one by one they jumped into the choppy waters of the Eastern Sea. The dog used all his strength and skill to keep afloat and to avoid the waves, so by the time the others had reached the shore he was still far out at sea. The Jade Emperor dispatched a prince of the Eastern Sea to help him but they could not prevent the grains from being washed off his body. Each wave that lashed his coat took a handful of rice along with it and to the Jade Emperor's dismay the grains were washed up on the shores of the island in the Eastern Sea.

When the dog finally lay exhausted on the shore of the earth only the grains that had stuck to his tail remained, just enough to plant a small patch of land. The field was ploughed and the rice planted by the people of the earth, but the gods had decided that life should not be too easy. The rice plants were no longer so heavily laden with grains as they had been on the gods' island, and now only sprouted grains at the tip of the stalk, so the people had to work twice as hard for their harvest.

From that time rice has been the staple crop of farmers throughout China and humans no longer need to risk their lives hunting in the forests. All the animals that swam to the earth have found work in the human world but dogs are the closest companions for the people who live on earth. They are even fed with rice at mealtimes as a reward for the service that they gave at the beginning of time. In some provinces dogs are fed with rice before being sold in the market, but horses, cows and sheep are only given straw and cocks and pigs are only thrown the husks.

Nu Wa Repairs the Sky

At one time the sky and the earth were still one. There was no sun and no moon. The wind, the rain and thunder had not yet been created, and mountains, rivers and trees had not yet taken shape. P'an Ku, the first being, gave life to this universe and created the natural features of the land.

From the moment of creation the sky and the earth grew apart from each other. After eighteen thousand years they had grown so far apart they could hardly be seen. P'an Ku studied the movement of the sky and afraid that it might one day fall to earth, attached a piece of hemp to each corner of the sky. He pulled the hemp ropes until the sky became taut and he knotted each rope firmly in a corner of the universe. To be extra sure that the sky would not collapse P'an Ku supported the four corners with thick wooden poles secured deep in the earth. At that time all that existed was Heaven, earth and P'an Ku. By the time he died, the sun and moon, the mountains and rivers, the rain and sunshine and all other natural phenomena had been created from his body and his breath.

As his final act P'an Ku created Nu Wa, the only woman on earth. She had a beautiful face and jet black hair but her body was made up of two long, black, knotted snakes. Her purpose on earth was to create perfect human beings who, unlike her, had bodies made of flesh and blood. Each day she mixed river mud and water into clay and meticulously moulded it into the shapes of men and women. Once her warm breath touched them they came alive.

One evening, while Nu Wa was resting beside a river bank, she found a piece of cord hidden in the reeds. She picked it up and dipped it into a muddy pool at her side. After a few seconds she took the cord out of the water and shook it dry. Each drop that fell on the grass glistened like a jewel for a moment and then immediately changed into a human being. Delighted to discover such a simple way to make humans, she created hundreds of people that very evening. This chance discovery made Nu Wa's life far easier, and during the following years she made millions of humans from drops of water, but she moulded very few from river clay. Those who had been formed by her hands were wise, courageous and wealthy, but those made of water were weak and timid.

Eventually Nu Wa was satisfied that she had created enough people to fill the earth, but it was only then that she realized how difficult it was to survive. The land was pitted with fiery volcanoes, the forests crowded with deadly animals and the rivers choked with dangerous fish. Although she was now growing old and weak she summoned to her all those she had created by hand and armed them with knives and spears. Together they travelled to every corner of the earth killing the wild animals, calming the volcanoes, damming the flood waters and clearing the forests. They made the earth hospitable for those who were too weak to defend themselves.

Out of the millions of people she had created Nu Wa saw that two men, Chuan Hsu and Kung Kung, were the most courageous. Both men were fighters and had been waging war against each other for many years. Nu Wa watched their battles with interest, although it hurt her to see how the land was scarred with their fighting and how the simple people made from drops of water died so quickly. One evening the two fighters came face to face and began a fight so vicious that the trees which stood in their way were sliced in half with one blow of their swords. By nightfall their wounds had formed a lake of blood, and it was Kung Kung who fell to his knees, unable to raise his sword in defence.

Kung Kung's pride and reputation had been destroyed and, knowing that he would lose face in his own town, he set off alone to the northwestern mountains of China. Even here in remote villages, he was recognized and ignored. He had no choice but to take his own life. He let himself fall into a rocky ravine cut into Pu Chou Shan Mountain and died when he hit the bottom. The force of his fall made the mountain reverberate and an avalanche of rocks came tumbling into the ravine, ripping up the trees that stood in its way. The avalanche gathered momentum on its course down the mountain and rolled towards the wooden poles supporting the sky at its northern and western corners. The poles snapped and the canopy of the sky fell towards the earth, ripping the hemp ropes as it descended. The sun was obliterated, the world sank into darkness, the wind rose and the rain poured through the crack in the sky. P'an Ku was distraught as he stood in Heaven and watched the devastation wrought upon his creation by human pride.

Meanwhile, back on earth, Nu Wa was furious that those she had created could not live in peace, and she was heartbroken to see her home devastated. Even though it was too late to change their character it was not too late to repair the damage to the earth. She caught and killed a turtle and planted its feet to mark the four corners of the earth so that she and everyone else on earth would always know in which direction they were facing. She then slaughtered a black dragon and used its body to block the flood of water pouring through the crack in the sky until she could find a stone of the right shape to plug the gap.

For months she desperately searched every corner of China for the ideal stone. As the days went by, the dragon's body began to sag under the weight of the water and the rain began to seep through the canopy of the sky. Finally, deep inside a mountain, she found a stone with a radiant quality and an inner spirit, and she knew at first glance that it was the stone that would repair the sky for eternity. Using fire, she carved the stone to the correct size. She lifted it to the heavens and, struggling against the torrent of water pouring through the tear, she slotted it into place.

Once more the sun rose in the heavens and the rain ceased. Nu Wa knew it was time to die, so she looked around for the bravest, strongest man on earth, and her gaze fell on Chuan Hsu. Before her death she appointed him her successor and gave him the title of Emperor. From that time on the Emperor of China was given the responsibility and the strength to maintain the harmony between Heaven and earth and the people who lived there.

The Water Ghost and the Fisherman

Water ghosts live in the depths of every river and sea in China. They are the spirits of unfortunate sailors, fishermen and people who have drowned and been dragged to the deepest, darkest waters, where they are fated to remain until they can find another human to take their place. Some water ghosts are luckier than others because their seas are so rough and dangerous that the unwary are continually being plunged to their deaths. As soon as a water ghost kills a person and drags his victim to the sea bed he can be reborn as a human and the new spirit must take his place.

The water ghost who lived in the river flowing beside the village of Hung Mao Pei was bored and dejected. He had been the local water ghost for as long as he could remember but the village was so small and peaceful that few people ventured onto the river, and when they did the water ghost always missed the opportunity to drown them. For many years the water ghost had been trying to kill Fung Hei, a wily and experienced fisherman, who sailed across the ghost's territory at least four times a week. The water ghost had whipped up storms, torn the fisherman's nets and bored a hole in his small fishing boat, but Fung Hei was too clever to be caught so easily.

One day the ghost spent ten hours driving the fish away from Fung Hei's net so that the fisherman would be forced to cast his nets late into the night. As the moon moved behind heavy clouds, the water ghost nimbly climbed aboard Fung Hei's boat and crouched in a dark corner near the helm, waiting for an opportune moment to kill the fisherman. He waited as Fung Hei sat silently staring into the deep waters, he heard the fisherman pray to the gods to grant him a catch, however small, and he watched the fisherman finish off the final grains of rice remaining in his wooden bowl. Finally, when the ghost was about to abandon hope, the fisherman leaned over the side of his boat to haul his nets aboard, and the ghost leaped up and pushed him into the dark, cold water.

For two minutes Fung Hei struggled and twisted against the ghost's vicious grip but eventually he lost consciousness. The delighted ghost pulled the fisherman's body to the river bank, smeared the dead man's face with river slime and placed a ghost tablet upon his tongue. After preparing the fisherman's body to enter the spirit world, the ghost flew as fast as he could to report his triumph to Yen Lo Wan, the Emperor of the Sea. But the ghost had anticipated his success, for the astute fisherman was not yet dead – the eager ghost had failed to hear the fisherman's slowly beating heart. The fisherman lay as though dead on the banks of the river until he was certain that the ghost had disappeared. Then he carefully placed the ghost tablet in his jacket pocket, washed the river slime off his face, ran to his home and bolted the door.

While all this was happening on earth Yen Lo Wan was listening to the water ghost's account of the fisherman's death and to his desperate plea for rebirth as a human. Yen Lo Wan rose from his magnificent golden throne and picked up the *Book of the Living and the Dead* from a coral table nearby. He scoured the pages showing the most recent water deaths but he could not find any record of the fisherman's death.

'Are you sure that this fisherman is dead?' demanded Yen Lo Wan.

'I'm absolutely certain,' cried the water ghost. 'How can any mortal survive more than three minutes under your waters?'

'This is the fourth time you've come to me with tales of death and once again you've made a fool of yourself,' roared the Sea Emperor. 'The fisherman is not dead. My scribes never make mistakes with their entries. Get back to your river immediately and retrieve your ghost tablet before you lose your chance of a human rebirth for ever.'

The crab guards were summoned to escort the distraught water ghost back to earth. The water ghost dashed back to the river bank where he had left the drowned fisherman but all that was left was the imprint of the fisherman's body in the mud. The unfortunate water ghost ran frantically from house to house in the village, peering through windows, squinting through cracks in the walls and knocking on doors, only to disappear when the owner appeared. Just before midnight, after an hour of fruitless searching, the water ghost found the fisherman's small wooden cottage. He rapped on the door until the fisherman was forced to leave his bed to see what was happening. The sleepy fisherman peered into the darkness but there was nobody there. He opened the door a little further to scan the small verandah in front of his house and there, slumped against a wooden post, he saw the water ghost sobbing.

'Please, I beg you, my fisherman brother, return my ghost tablet, otherwise I will never live on this earth again,' pleaded the ghost.

The fisherman was touched by the ghost's plight. He ran into his house and returned carrying the priceless ghost tablet. But he was only willing to return it on condition the ghost would regularly fill his nets with fish. The ghost grudgingly agreed.

From that day onwards the fisherman's catch increased tenfold. The boat was often so heavy with fish that the fisherman feared he would not reach the river bank safely. At first the water ghost always remained just below the surface when he drove the fish in the fisherman's direction, but gradually he began to appear above the surface to chat to the fisherman. Before long the two became good friends and exactly a month after their first meeting the fisherman invited the ghost to his house for an evening meal. The water ghost and the fisherman enjoyed each other's company so much that they began to meet twice a week to share dinner in the fisherman's cottage.

Early one morning the water ghost rushed into the fisherman's house and took his friend by the arm. 'I am sorry to tell you this, but today I must leave you. This afternoon an old woman will walk along the muddy banks of the river and with a little push from me she will fall and drown in the deep waters. It's an ideal opportunity to change my fate. You've been a good friend and I'm sorry to leave you, but this is the way it must be.'

'Wait one moment,' cried the fisherman. 'I know how important it is for you to escape from the spirit world, but you can't kill an innocent old woman. How can you submit her to such a cold, painful death? And furthermore, who will help me with my fishing? Without you I will barely survive.'

Over the months the water ghost had grown to care deeply for his new friend, and so he sat down at the fisherman's table to think this problem through. For a long time the two men sat in silence. Finally the water ghost spoke up and agreed with the fisherman, saying he would delay his departure for at least three years.

The water ghost kept his promise and for three years nobody drowned in the river. Each day they met upon the lake and during festivals the water ghost would stay in the fisherman's house. But the time came when the water ghost decided to drown an unwary swimmer and once more he confided in the fisherman.

'Tomorrow a young boy will go swimming in the river and I will pull him down to the river bed. Don't try to stop me this time. I can't live in this miserable river for ever.'

The fisherman didn't say anything. He just gazed at the floor and sadly shook his head. The ghost turned his back on the fisherman and quietly left the cottage.

The next morning the fisherman rowed out to the middle of the river as usual. Just as he was about to lower his nets he spotted a young boy skipping beside the river bank. The fisherman dropped his nets, grabbed his oars and raced to the bank where the boy was paddling in the water.

'Go home this minute,' cried the fisherman. 'Your mother needs you urgently. If you don't go now she'll beat you for being lazy.'

The startled young boy ran home immediately and the satisfied fisherman returned to his nets.

That evening the furious water ghost called at the fisherman's house, but the fisherman had anticipated his arrival and prepared a table brimming with succulent meat and fish. As soon as the ghost entered the room the fisherman began his apology.

'I'm sorry, my friend, I know you're unhappy in the river, but that young boy has a fortunate life ahead of him. Please don't blame me. I'll never interfere in your plans again.'

Placated by the fisherman's words and tempted by the meal, the water ghost sat down to share the food. The matter was never mentioned again.

Several years passed and the two remained firm friends, but one day, during dinner at the fisherman's house, the ghost lost his patience and declared that the time had come for him to leave the river. Under pressure from the fisherman the water ghost reluctantly revealed his plan.

'You know that I care for you very much, but compare the way you live to my miserable life on the cold river bed. Unless I do something to help myself I will live there for all eternity. When you die I won't have a friend in the world, so I must do something now to save myself. I heard your neighbour, Chang Shan, quarrelling violently with her husband. I sense she will commit suicide in the river tomorrow morning. This time I am not going to kill anyone. She is dying by her own hand, so you can't blame me.'

The fisherman was shocked to hear this news and under his breath he vowed to help Chang Shan although he had promised the ghost not to interfere again. That night the fisherman lay awake thinking about the task ahead of him. By daybreak he had decided to risk his friendship with the water ghost and save the woman from suicide. Without stopping to wash, eat or brush his hair, the fisherman dressed as fast as he could and rushed down to the river. He arrived just in time to see Mrs Chang throw herself into a dangerous whirlpool and he dived in after her. The powerful currents pulled them downwards and finally she lost consciousness in the fisherman's arms, but the fisherman swam with all his might in his efforts to save them both. The water ghost watched eagerly in the shadows but didn't attempt to save them or to kill them. He waited for fate to take its course. After a long fight against the strong currents of the river the brave fisherman pulled Mrs Chang ashore and carried her home to her distressed husband.

That night there was a knock on the door. Without waiting for an answer, the water ghost timidly entered the room and sat at the kitchen table without saying a word. The fisherman attempted to offer an explanation but the water ghost stopped him before he could begin.

'I haven't come here to blame you or to shout at you. I

know exactly why you saved that woman and I realize that you didn't make that decision lightly. I know that you care for me but I also know you care for human life, and that is why I promise never to kill anyone or let them kill themselves to satisfy my needs. What the gods have bestowed, I accept.'

When he heard the ghost's words the fisherman knew that the water ghost was the greatest friend that he would ever make during his lifetime.

After this incident the water ghost and the fisherman passed many happy hours eating, talking, playing cards and fishing together. Ten years passed since their first meeting and the water ghost had not harmed any living creature.

Meanwhile in the Sea Emperor's palace Yen Lo Wan was keeping a careful check on his subjects' characters and behaviour. While all the other water ghosts and spirits under his command had regularly drowned unfortunate victims, the water ghost of Hung Mao Pei had never troubled any of the humans who ventured onto his territory. The water ghost had accepted his fortune with a humility that surprised even the Emperor. After calling his advisors to a council meeting in the Sea Palace, the Emperor recommended the water ghost to the Jade Emperor, and in turn the Jade Emperor decided to promote the water ghost to Ch'eng Huang, the district god.

One autumn evening, as the water ghost rose from the depths of the lake to visit the fisherman, he was approached by the Jade Emperor's vizier bearing a promotion order. The water ghost was overcome with delight and rushed to the fisherman's cottage brandishing his promotion papers. But the fisherman had not returned from market and the water ghost had no time to waste, so he left an invitation card to his new temple and flew off eagerly to take up his prestigious appointment.

When the fisherman returned at dusk he discovered the invitation but was convinced that this respected god had

made a mistake. For many days the fisherman was un-
decided what to do but as the day of the appointment
approached he decided to accept the invitation. From the
day the fisherman found the invitation upon his kitchen
table he had not seen the water ghost. Every day he went
down to the river and called to his friend deep in the
waters, but there was no reply. Each evening he waited
for his friend to knock on his cottage door, but he never
arrived. Day by day the fisherman's catch grew smaller,
but that was nothing compared to the loss of his friend.

At the arranged hour the fisherman arrived at Ch'eng
Huang Temple, but the grounds and the temple itself
were empty. It was almost dusk and a light wind blew
between the ornate pillars and rustled the leaves strewn
across the temple lawn. The fisherman was exhausted
after his journey so he cleared the leaves from a stone
bench outside the temple door, spread his cotton jacket
upon the bench and fell into a deep sleep. In his dreams
he saw his friend the water ghost wearing the robes of
Ch'eng Huang. His friend approached him and handed
him a golden dish laden with aromatic meats and rare
fish. The water ghost stood by silently while the ravenous
fisherman ate the food. The water ghost then placed a
heavy bag of gold coins in the fisherman's lap and afterwards bowed down before the fisherman.

'If it had not been for you, my most trusted friend, I
would have killed many people, but you saved me and I
now bow down before you in thanks. I can no longer help
you to fish but I can give you gold which you must spend
wisely. You will never see me again but I will always think
of you.'

The water ghost then faded from the fisherman's
dream.

It was nearly daybreak when the fisherman awoke. As
he slowly stood up to gather his jacket and leave the
temple, a bag of gold fell to the floor.

The fisherman invested his gift wisely and became a

prosperous businessman. From that day on he never again fished in the river and nobody ever drowned in its waters, but each day he went down to the river bank and offered prayers to Ch'eng Huang.

The Spotted Deer and the Tiger

Yu Yu, the spotted deer, usually grazed on the outskirts of a dense forest. He had never ventured beyond the line of banyan trees that marked the forest boundary. One day a farmer's dog wandered into the grazing lands and began to chase Yu Yu. The timid deer had never been threatened before and he ran, petrified, into the forest. In the unexpected darkness he ran blindly into overhanging creepers, charged head first into thick tree trunks and fell into mossy ditches. When his eyes were eventually adjusted to the forest shadows he tried to find his way back to the grazing lands but he only stumbled deeper and deeper into the unknown, terrifying forest.

When Yu Yu finally stopped to rest, a porcupine shuffled towards him from the undergrowth and tentatively sniffed his hooves. The porcupine raised its long nose into the air to investigate this strange animal and demanded sharply, 'Who are you and what are you doing here?'

'My name is Yu Yu. I am a spotted deer,' replied Yu Yu gently.

He had hardly finished speaking when a pheasant flew down, brushing its wings against his antlers.

'So you're a spotted deer. I've heard talk of them. Do they all look as strange as you?'

'Yes, I'm a spotted deer and all spotted deer look like me. Haven't you ever seen one before?'

'No, I can't say we have. They've never ventured into our forest before,' shouted a snail resting on a pine leaf above Yu Yu's head.

Yu Yu looked inquiringly at his audience before he spoke. 'Please help me. I need you to teach me about life in the forest.'

The forest animals did not hesitate to offer this timid newcomer their help. After suggesting good food to eat and safe places to rest, they left Yu Yu to discover the variety of forest life.

Some hours later Yu Yu entered a clearing. As he raised his head to look around he found himself gazing directly into the hard, glistening green eyes of a tiger. Yu Yu was panic stricken. He knew that the tiger could kill him with one blow of its powerful paws. But fortunately the tiger did not move a muscle. He had never seen a spotted deer before and was intrigued by its unusual shape.

'Why are you so ugly?' demanded the tiger.

Yu Yu was quivering with fear but he mustered all his strength and replied confidently, 'I am Yu Yu, the spotted deer.'

'Oh, so you're a spotted deer,' growled the tiger. 'Well, tell me, what are those plants growing out of the top of your head?'

While Yu Yu was desperately thinking of a convincing answer the tiger slunk towards him. Just as Yu Yu was about to collapse with terror he hit upon a clever idea.

'You're not a very intelligent animal, are you?' he replied scornfully. 'You mean to tell me that you don't know what these simple things are? As you obviously lack the most basic education I had better tell you what they are. They are tiger chopsticks. Because tiger meat is so smooth I have to eat it with curved chopsticks to prevent the meat slipping back into my bowl.'

The tiger stepped back in shock. In all his years of stalking and hunting he had never heard of anyone who dared eat tiger meat and he was disgusted and startled by the thought of it. He sidled closer to Yu Yu to assess his adversary's strength and stamina.

'You're too small to kill a tiger,' he said.

Yu Yu's eyes rounded in amazement. 'What do you mean, I'm too small to kill a tiger?' said Yu Yu scornfully. 'Just look at these spots on my back. You obviously don't know what they are. They represent the number of tigers that I've killed and eaten. Three years ago I went to visit the Jade Emperor to find out how I could become immortal and he gave me a mission on earth. He told me to kill every tiger that has eaten living flesh, and for each tiger I will receive a spot. When I have killed a thousand tigers I will become immortal. Now see if you can work out how many spots there are on my body?' As Yu Yu spoke he began to quiver and then he started to shake violently.

Once again the tiger grew suspicious. 'If you are able to kill and eat tigers, why are you trembling?'

'I'm not trembling,' replied Yu Yu with an unsteady voice. 'Before I eat a tiger I have to build up my energy. I'm quivering with force, not with fear.'

The tiger didn't wait to hear any more. He just turned on his heels and fled into the thick undergrowth without a backward glance. He ran and ran until he was sure that the deer had lost track of him, and then he fell down breathlessly under the branches of a pine tree.

'Hello, King Tiger,' cried a voice from an overhanging branch. 'You're obviously trying to escape from someone. Who are you afraid of?'

The tiger looked up and was greeted by the smiling face of a monkey who was hanging upside down from a branch. The monkey was interested in hearing the tiger's

story so he unwound his tail from the branch, jumped
down to the forest floor and settled himself at the tiger's
feet. Stammering and stuttering, the tiger revealed his
strange story but the monkey only stared in disbelief.
After hearing a full account of the adventure the monkey
demanded to be taken to the spotted deer.

'No, I refuse to go,' snapped the tiger. 'What if the deer
attacks me? I've no escape. At least you can climb up a
tree to safety.'

But the monkey would not take no for an answer and
cajoled and begged until the tiger finally agreed to take
him to the deer on one condition. The monkey had to be
strapped to the tiger's back so that when the monkey
escaped by swinging on a branch he would carry the tiger
up with him. As soon as the monkey was securely tied to
the tiger's back with thick creepers they made their way
back to the clearing.

Yu Yu lifted his head as he heard a rustle not far away
in the shadowy undergrowth and then he caught a glimpse
of the tiger's stripes lit by a shaft of sunlight. Yu Yu
jumped back in surprise and the tiger froze in fright. He
thought that the deer was summoning up every ounce of
energy to kill him and once again he turned on his heels
and ran for his life. He charged blindly through bushes,
thorns and ditches and all the time the helpless monkey
was strapped to his back. The monkey eventually fainted
and before long the tiger himself collapsed on the forest
floor. When the tiger finally recovered his breath he turned
to the monkey.

'I warned you,' he snapped. 'I told you how ferocious
the spotted deer is, but you wouldn't believe me.' From
that day on the monkey spent his time in the topmost
branches of the trees and the tiger rarely left the depths
of the forest.

Kuan Yin's Prophecy

The Lo Yang river was the busiest, widest and most dangerous in Fukien province. It was the main highway for the barges carrying food and raw materials throughout the province, but many people had died trying to cross its turbulent waters and every attempt to build a bridge had failed.

Early one autumn morning, without warning, the area around the Lo Yang river was struck by a storm so strong that it ripped trees from the ground and demolished huts with one gust of wind. A small passenger ship trying to cross the river was being dragged into whirlpools and then lifted out by the ferocity of the wind and thrown on its side by waves high enough to block the dawn light. Passengers screamed for help, children cried with fear, and baskets of chickens, fish and vegetables were thrown across the deck and into the water.

Just as the passengers began to give up hope of ever walking on land again, the tall figure of a woman in a white dress appeared on the prow of the ship. She closed her eyes and raised her arms to the waters which bowed to her command. The winds ceased, the waves subsided and the storm clouds cleared. The passengers stared in disbelief at Kuan Yin, the Goddess of Mercy, and one by one they fell to their knees and bowed their heads low before her.

Kuan Yin walked slowly across the ship and approached a pregnant woman crouched near the ship's rail. 'Fong Ts'ai, you have no need to thank me, for you will bear a child who will build a bridge to cross the Lo Yang river.'

After making this prophecy Kuan Yin disappeared and the amazed crowd gathered round Fong Ts'ai to congratulate her. Stunned but elated by Kuan Yin's words, Fong Ts'ai returned home and not long afterwards gave birth to a boy whom she named Ts'ai Hsiang.

Ts'ai Hsiang grew up to be a good and obedient son. By the age of seven he was helping his mother on her small plot of land and soon he was running it completely.

Each year, on the eve of his birthday, his mother reminded him of Kuan Yin's prophecy. 'Remember, my son, when you grow up you must build a bridge over the Lo Yang river. Never let anything or anyone stand in your way.'

Each year Ts'ai Hsiang listened respectfully and vowed to fulfil this prophecy.

At the age of thirty Ts'ai Hsiang passed an examination to work for the government and after years of dedicated work he was promoted to the post of Prime Minister. Even though wealth and honours were heaped on him by the Emperor there was always a nagging thought at the back of his mind. He had administered the provinces wisely and he was well respected by peasants and nobles alike, but he had not built the prophesied bridge. Year after year he put forward reasons for visiting Fukien province, but each time the Emperor refused to let his wise Prime Minister leave his side.

One evening, as Ts'ai Hsiang was resting in the Imperial Gardens, he noticed a line of ants marching into a hole in the rockery and he hit upon a plan. Early the next morning he returned to the Imperial Gardens carrying a stick smeared with honey. After making sure that he was alone in the garden he inscribed eight Chinese characters in honey on the leaves of a plantain tree. The characters read, 'Ts'ai Hsiang, Ts'ai Hsiang, return home to fulfil your duty.'

Ts'ai Hsiang returned to his room overlooking the palace gardens and within five minutes the ants had clambered onto the plantain tree to eat the honey. Half an hour later the Emperor entered the garden for his early-morning stroll. As he wandered around examining the flowers and plants he spotted the line of ants forming eight characters on the plantain tree and he read the words out loud.

This was the moment Ts'ai Hsiang had been waiting for and he ran into the garden and bowed low before the Emperor. 'Thank you, Your Majesty!' he cried. 'I'll return home tomorrow.'

The Emperor drew back in surprise and ordered Ts'ai Hsiang to rise to his feet. 'What are you talking about?' he demanded. 'I haven't ordered you to return home. I was only reading the characters out loud.'

But Ts'ai Hsiang was not to be defeated and he argued his case impatiently. 'Your Majesty, everyone in the kingdom knows that your word is the Imperial will, and once you have spoken your will must be carried out.'

The Emperor had no choice but to agree. Unwillingly, he gave his Prime Minister permission to return home for two months to work as the magistrate of Ch'uan Ch'ou village.

From the moment Ts'ai Hsiang returned, a gang of workmen was employed to build the bridge, but the foundation stones were continually being washed away like pebbles by the powerful river currents. Time was running short for Ts'ai Hsiang and in desperation he composed a

letter to the Sea Dragon King begging him to hold back
the turbulent waters for three days.

As soon as the letter had been written and sealed with
the Prime Minister's symbol, Ts'ai Hsiang went in search
of a messenger among his workmen. 'Who will go down
to the sea?' demanded Ts'ai Hsiang. One unfortunate
workman, Hsia Te Hai, misheard the question and
thought he was being summoned to the magistrate's presence. 'Here I am, here I am,' announced the eager
workman.

'Well done,' congratulated Ts'ai Hsiang. 'Go to the
depths of the Lo Yang river and hand this letter to the Sea
Dragon King.' And he handed the bewildered workman a
sealed parchment letter.

Hsia Te Hai was escorted to the muddy banks of the
Lo Yang river by his work companions and left alone as
darkness fell. When everyone had disappeared from sight
Hsia Te Hai fell to his knees and wept in fear and panic.
When he had finally exhausted himself he fell asleep by
the river. In his dream he was standing in the pearl- and
shell-encrusted hall of the Sea Dragon King's palace. To
his right a crab general was giving orders to his prawn
soldiers and to his left sat the Sea Dragon King upon a
golden throne. Hsia Te Hai rushed to the base of the
throne and prostrated himself at the king's feet.

'My, my . . . name is . . . Hsia Te Hai,' he stammered.
'This letter . . . is for you . . . Sea Dragon . . . Sea Dragon
King.'

The Sea Dragon King took the letter from Hsia Te
Hai's outstretched hand and slowly read it.

'I can do what the Prime Minister requested,' replied
the king. 'I promise to move the water for three days, but
no longer.'

The Sea Dragon King then inscribed a Chinese character on Hsia Te Hai's palm and waved him out of his
presence. Without daring to look into the face of this

powerful king the humble workman left the palace as quickly as possible.

A sharp morning wind woke Hsia Te Hai from his vivid dream, and as he pulled himself up from the damp river bank he caught a glimpse of a Chinese character inscribed on his palm. The events of his dream came flooding back to him and he ran through the early-morning mist to the house where Ts'ai Hsiang was sleeping. Hsia Te Hai pushed back the guards who blocked his path and forced his way into his master's chamber.

'Master forgive me for disturbing your sleep, but I have spoken with the Sea Dragon King,' he cried excitedly, 'and this is the message he sent you.' Hsia Te Hai laid his hand upon the silk bedcovers while Ts'ai Hsiang deciphered the following words: 'The 21st day at Yu hours.'

And so, on the 21st day of that month at six o'clock in the evening, a mighty roar could be heard throughout Ch'uan Ch'ou village as the waters of the Lo Yang river were pushed aside to reveal the rocky river bed. Before picking up their tools Ts'ai Hsiang and his workmen burned incense and paper money as an offering to the Sea Dragon King and then, with a vow not to rest until he had finished his task, Ts'ai Hsiang ordered his men to work. The river was more than a mile wide, and although a thousand men had been employed to carry out the work, at the end of the first day only a third of the work had been completed and the food rations had been completely exhausted. No matter how much Ts'ai Hsiang threatened or cajoled his workmen, they refused to work until they saw fresh food rations. Just when all seemed lost Ts'ai Hsiang remembered Kuan Yin, the Goddess of Mercy, who had saved his mother's life. He fell to his knees and prayed fervently.

'Kuan Yin, you told my mother that I would build the bridge and I want to fulfil your wish, but I need more money to buy food for my workmen. Goddess of Mercy, please bestow your wisdom on me. Help me when I most need you.'

The following day a rowing boat appeared on the Lo Yang river and in its prow sat a beautiful woman in a white silk dress. Word of her beauty soon passed among the villagers and they hurried down the valley to catch a glimpse of her. The woman drew her boat close to the jostling crowd and hushed their excited murmurs with a slight movement of her hand. When every gaze was fixed attentively upon her, she spoke.

'I promise to marry the man who can throw a gold or silver coin into my lap.' No sooner had she finished speaking than she was showered with so many coins that the boat began to sink, but no matter how carefully the villagers aimed, no one could throw a coin into her lap. An hour later, when the boat could not bear the weight of another coin, the woman told the villagers to return to their homes. As Ts'ai Hsiang turned to make his way back to the village the woman summoned him to her side.

'Ts'ai Hsiang, I heard your prayers and I have come to help you. This money is yours and you must use it to fulfil my prophecy.'

Kuan Yin poured the money onto the grass at Ts'ai Hsiang's feet and then, without another word, she disappeared to Heaven in a twist of green smoke.

Without wasting a moment Ts'ai Hsiang sent his men back to work. Under Ts'ai Hsiang's tireless and determined command they worked ceaselessly, and an hour before the Sea Dragon King freed the mighty waters the bridge was completed.

The Barber and the Immortal

Wang San worked as a roadside barber. He was skilled and efficient, and ready to help anyone in need, but the people of the town despised him because of his lowly position.

One day Wang San was approached by two of the Emperor's guards and ordered to present himself at the Imperial Palace the following day to cut the Emperor's hair. The Emperor's head was misshapen and pitted with purulent sores and deep scars, which even the most skilled physicians had failed to cure. Every barber who accidentally drew blood from the Emperor's scalp was beheaded immediately – thus many talented barbers had entered the palace but few had left. Wang San knew the dreadful fate that lay ahead of him and turned to his neighbours for support, but instead of offering consolation they took pleasure in his misfortune. He heard the villagers whispering about him in the narrow lanes and dark doorways of the village and children ran after him shouting that his time had come.

That night Wang San paced the earthen floor of his

43

wooden hut for hours on end. While the villagers slept he sharpened his razor again and again until its fine cutting edge was wafer thin. He laid the razor upon a table, lit three incense sticks in front of his household shrine and fell on his knees in front of the gods.

'Heavenly Immortals, please help me!' he cried. 'I have no one to turn to but you.'

At that very moment Lu Tung Pin, one of the Eight Immortals, was flying through the darkness above Peking, and he heard Wang San's desperate plea rising through the still night air. As Lu Tung Pin descended to earth Wang San slumped exhausted to the floor and in a dream he heard Lu Tung Pin's reassuring voice.

'Do not worry, Wang San: Tomorrow, as you're approaching the palace gates, a man will appear beside you who will be identical to you. When you see this man you must disappear as quickly as possible into the nearby gardens.'

In his dream Wang San warned Lu Tung Pin about the Emperor's heartless punishment for those who drew blood from his scalp, but Lu Tung Pin allayed his fears. The voice of the immortal faded from the dream and Wang San fell into a deep sleep.

When Wang San awoke he remembered the dream very clearly, but he did not know whether to believe what he had heard. After a meagre breakfast, the frightened barber slung his toolbox over his shoulder and, with a heavy heart, set out for his appointment. He passed quickly through the village, ignoring the taunts of his neighbours, and headed for the palace. As Lu Tung Pin had promised, he was approached by a man who looked exactly like him and who carried an identical toolbox. The stranger turned to wink at Wang San and then swaggered towards the guards at the palace gates. For a moment Wang San stood gazing after him and then, for fear that his luck should turn, he ran to hide in the nearby gardens, then secretly made his way home.

Lu Tung Pin had fulfilled his promise and, in the guise of the barber, he was ushered into the Emperor's presence. After bowing in front of the Emperor, Lu Tung Pin prepared his razor, mixed a bowl of shaving cream and ordered the guards to bring hot towels. The Emperor was impressed by his confidence and efficiency and felt secure when he sensed Lu Tung Pin's steady hand working across his scalp.

'Most barbers who cut my hair are always trembling. I find it strange that your hand is as steady as a rock!' exclaimed the Emperor.

'That's because not only am I a good barber, but I also have the power to heal your sores and smooth your scars,' replied Lu Tung Pin confidently.

The Emperor warned Lu Tung Pin of his fate if one drop of blood should appear on the hot towels, but the barber did not flinch. As soon as the razor touched the Emperor's sores and scars the infections dried up and the scars miraculously healed.

The Emperor was delighted with the barber's skill. 'I never imagined anyone could cure me so painlessly. As a measure of my thanks you can have as much gold as you can carry.'

'With all due respect, Your Majesty, I am not interested in gold,' replied Lu Tung Pin modestly. 'All that I want is a red Imperial flag as a sign of your favour.'

His request was granted and Lu Tung Pin returned to Wang San's house bearing the red Imperial flag. He found Wang San shaking feverishly on his bed and he gently laid the flag upon his damp pillow.

'You need never fear the Emperor again,' Lu Tung Pin assured him. 'You have honoured the immortals throughout your life and that is why I arrived to help you. Place this red flag outside your door. It will bring you good fortune.'

Lu Tung Pin disappeared as quickly and as quietly as he had come.

Wang San fixed the red flag above the door of his hut and from that day onwards customers were drawn to his house, reassured by this symbol of royal appointment. Other barbers, jealous of Wang San's popularity, copied his example and also hung red flags outside their shops to attract customers. That is why, to this day, there are red flags hanging outside barber's shops throughout China.

The Merchant's Revenge

At the age of fifteen Liu Shih Ch'ang left his impoverished family to search for work in a nearby city. He became an apprentice to a silk merchant and through hard work and natural talent he grew knowledgeable, well known and respected. By the age of thirty he was one of the wealthiest silk merchants in the province, but he had not forgotten his roots and vowed to return to his family to support them in their old age.

One spring morning he loaded two horses with gold, jade, ivory and gifts of silk and set out to visit his parents. At nightfall he was still half a day's journey from his home village and so he decided to find an inn for the night. After searching fruitlessly for several hours he saw a lantern hanging over the door of a potterymaker and he knocked at the door in search of a bed.

Unfortunately he had chosen the house of the greediest couple in the village. As soon as they opened the door the potter and his wife noted the merchant's expensive clothes and heavy bags bulging with precious goods, strapped to his horses' backs. The temptation to steal these goods was too great for such an avaricious couple and as soon as the merchant sat down to eat a bowl of rice Ch'au T'ai hit Liu Shih Ch'ang so hard with an iron hammer that his skull cracked open. Under cover of darkness the murderous couple carried the merchant's body into a field behind their house and carefully buried it in a deep grave.

News of the potterymaker's sudden wealth travelled quickly through the district and soon reached the ears of a moneylender, Chang Pieh Ku. He immediately saddled his horse and set off to reclaim the potter's outstanding loan. When Chang Pieh Ku arrived at his debtor's house he could not believe the changes that had been made to the potterymaker's home. Two new bedrooms with an intricate wrought-iron verandah had been built and a rock garden and fish pool had been created in the once overgrown garden. Although extravagant changes had been made to the house and the garden, not one bowl, jug or pot had been sold in the pottery shop. In fact, it had been so long since the shop had opened to the public that a layer of dust now covered the earthenware dishes.

Chang Pieh Ku knocked on the shop door and was warmly greeted by the potter.

'Welcome to my home. I think I can guess why you're here. You'd like to borrow money from me, am I right?' inquired the potter.

'What do you mean, borrow money from you?' said Chang Pieh Ku in astonishment. 'Surely you haven't forgotten your debt?'

'Now, my good friend,' replied the potter. 'There's no need to be ashamed of your poverty. I know you're asking for charity. There's no need to pretend that I owe you money.'

'What do you mean by that? You know very well that I lent you enough money to buy food supplies for the winter. I'm not moving from this spot until you repay your debt,' answered the moneylender defiantly.

But the potter refused and the two men stood locked in silence.

Finally the potter opened the drawstring of a leather bag hanging at his waist. 'Here, take this and go. Be grateful for my charity.' And he emptied a mound of coins upon the floor and watched Chang Pieh Ku reluctantly crawl on his hands and knees as he gathered them up.

After counting the coins Chang Pieh Ku was still short of the full amount, so he picked up an earthenware dish to compensate for the discrepancy. He placed the dish under his coat, left the shop in a furious temper and headed for his home on the far side of a forest. Halfway through the forest the trees were stirred by a bitter wind which cut through his thin cotton jacket. The cold seemed to reach his bones and first he shivered and then he sneezed. He sneezed with such force that the earthenware dish slipped from his inside pocket and fell to the forest floor.

'Ow, be careful! That hurt!' cried a voice nearby.

Chang Pieh Ku glanced around to see where the voice came from but all he could hear was the whistling of the wind in the trees.

Convinced that he was imagining things, Chang Pieh Ku continued on his way, but the same voice demanded that he slow down. Chang Pieh Ku ignored the voice and made his way home as quickly as possible. When he entered his kitchen he threw the earthenware dish onto a wooden chair and again the voice cried out in pain. This time Chang Pieh Ku was sure that the voice came from the earthenware dish, so he picked it up and held it to his ear.

'Yes, I'm in the earthenware dish!' cried the voice in desperation. 'Please help me, Chang, I've been murdered. Help me to bring my murderer to justice.'

'Are you a ghost?' asked Chang Pieh Ku, but the dish remained silent. He persisted with his questioning. 'What type of spirit are you? Why are you hiding in this earthenware dish and who murdered you?'

Liu Shih Ch'ang revealed how he had been murdered and buried in the potter's back garden. Liu Shih Ch'ang's soul had entered the red clay earth in which the grave had been dug and several days after the murder the potter had used this clay to make an earthenware dish. This was the same dish that Chang Pieh Ku now held in his hands. The spirit needed a human to help him report this crime to Pao Kung, the district judge. When the spirit had finished talking, tears fell from the dish. Startled at the spectacle of a weeping dish, Chang Pieh Ku agreed to bring the potter to justice and at daybreak the following morning he carefully wrapped the dish in a silk cloth and set out for the people's court in the nearest city.

When he arrived at the gates of the magistrate's court he recounted with great urgency the story of the earthenware dish and was immediately ushered into Pao Kung's presence.

The wise judge listened patiently to the story and then asked the soul in the dish to identify itself. But Liu Shih Ch'ang's soul didn't utter a single syllable. Pao Kung lifted the dish up to his ear and asked again, 'Soul of the dish, speak to me.'

But once again the dish remained silent.

Pao Kung presumed that the moneylender had become senile and ordered his guards to escort him into the street. Angry and humiliated, Chang Pieh Ku slapped the dish hard and demanded that Liu Shih Ch'ang explain his silence in front of the judge.

'Please don't hit me. I couldn't reply because I wasn't there. The two guards at the gate allowed you in but the door gods of the spirit world wouldn't let me pass through. Can you explain this to Pao Kung?'

Chang Pieh Ku returned to the judge, who again listened sympathetically and then drew a charm requesting the door gods to grant right of entry. The court guards burned the charm outside the gates and Liu Shih Ch'ang's spirit was allowed to enter the court inside the earthenware dish. Chang Pieh Ku placed the dish on the judge's desk and once again asked the spirit of the dish to speak. But again the dish remained silent. Chang Pieh Ku grew impatient and shook the dish violently. Still the spirit of the dish failed to reply.

Pao Kung was convinced that the whole episode was a plot to make him look foolish and he summoned the court guards to his office with orders to soundly beat the moneylender and throw him into the street.

The guards' leather whips lacerated Chang Pieh Ku's skin and he lay till sunset at the side of the road outside the palace. When he came to his senses he slowly pulled himself to his feet and vehemently kicked the earthenware dish into the gutter.

'Calm down, please. I can explain everything,' shouted the spirit. 'Please just give me one more chance,' begged Liu Shih Ch'ang. 'I was just about to speak to the judge when I remembered that I was naked. I couldn't speak to the judge with a naked body. My spirit must be clothed to show due respect. Please don't abandon me when I most need you. Without your help I will be trapped in this dish for all eternity. Please give me one more chance, please save me.'

Chang Pieh Ku didn't have the heart to refuse Liu Shih Ch'ang's pleas and he grudgingly agreed to help him one more time. He placed a cloth around the dish and limped back to the court gates, calling out Liu Shih Ch'ang's name every few yards to ensure he was still there.

'Stop worrying,' replied the spirit. 'I am still here and I promise to remain here.'

When they reached the gates, Liu Shih Ch'ang's spirit ordered the guards to stand aside. The guards were so surprised to hear a speaking dish that they immediately jumped out of the way.

Chang Pieh Ku ran to Pao Kung's office and laid the

cloth-wrapped dish on the judge's desk. 'Ask him anything you want,' he cried breathlessly.

'Get out of my sight,' the judge ordered angrily.

'Your Honour, listen to the dish. Please hear what it has to say.'

No sooner had Chang Pieh Ku finished speaking than a plaintive voice from the dish eloquently described the events leading up to Liu Shih Ch'ang's murder. The spirit paused for comment from the judge, but Pao Kung was too stunned to speak, so the spirit continued the story unabashed. At length the spirit finished describing the events of the merchant's death and without hesitation Pao Kung summoned the guards to arrest the potter and his wife.

The following morning the murderers were brought to the court and the spirit of the dish gave evidence against them. When the dish had finished speaking the potter's wife collapsed in tears and admitted their crime. A guilty verdict was given and the death sentence passed. That evening, as the sun was setting, they were hanged in the town square before a jeering crowd.

After the hanging Chang Pieh Ku returned home weary from his adventure but satisfied with the outcome. The dish had not spoken since the hanging, so Chang Pieh Ku presumed that Liu Shih Ch'ang's spirit was resting and he carefully placed the dish on the highest shelf in his kitchen. Under the judge's orders Chang Pieh Ku gave the potter's estate and all their belongings to Liu Shih Ch'ang's parents and the grateful parents granted him a large reward. Chang Pieh Ku placed his reward of gold, silver and jade in a leather bag and buried it beneath the kitchen floorboards. As soon as he put the floor boards back in place the dish jumped off the shelf and fell to the floor. Chang Pieh Ku meticulously glued the broken pieces together but the dish never spoke again. Liu Shih Ch'ang's spirit had finally escaped.

Chang Ku Lao's Test

Chang Ku Lao was a wise old man with a quick mind, but his three sons were slow and foolish. His two oldest sons had married women who turned out to be equally stupid. He knew that they were too foolish to take care of themselves and he worried about what would happen to them after his death. He eventually decided to find an intelligent girl who would make a good wife for his dim-witted youngest son, but however hard he searched he was unable to find a suitable match. Concerned for the future of his family, he devised a plan to test his daughters-in-law, hoping to uncover a spark of intelligence in their characters.

One summer's morning the old man summoned both the girls for a meeting. 'It's a long time since you have both seen your parents and I suspect that you must be missing them very much. Am I right?'

The girls nodded in agreement and the old man continued, 'Both of you must pack your bags immediately and go visit them, but you must return when I tell you to. You, my elder daughter-in-law, can stay three five days and

53

you, my younger daughter-in-law, can stay seven eight days.'

The girls were so excited they nodded vigorously in agreement without considering what he had said.

Just as they were leaving the room Chang Ku Lao made another request. 'I would like you both to return with a gift for me. One of you must return with a paper-wrapped fire and the other must return with a legless chicken.'

By now the girls were so eager to leave they immediately agreed to this request. Only when the girls were saying goodbye to each other on the road outside their village did they realize what they had agreed to.

'I've been told to return in three five days with a paper-wrapped fire but I haven't any idea what he means!' exclaimed the elder daughter-in-law.

'Well, I'm just as confused as you,' replied the youngest daughter-in-law. 'I don't know what he expects me to do and if I don't return at the right time with the right present he will think I'm stupid.'

The two girls sat and discussed these riddles until their heads ached but they still could not find an answer. Eventually the younger daughter-in-law began to cry and before long the elder daughter-in-law was unable to control her tears. As the two girls sat weeping a pork butcher and his daughter, Fung Ku, passed by.

Fung Ku approached the distraught girls. 'What's wrong, why are you crying so much? Have you been hurt?'

'No, it's far worse than that,' replied the elder daughter-in-law. 'We can't return home until we find a solution to our problem.'

In between sobs the girls told Fung Ku everything that had happened.

'There's no reason to cry,' said Fung Ku reassuringly. 'The answer is easy. Three multiplied by five is fifteen and seven plus eight is fifteen – after fifteen days you must return home. Don't worry about the present either. A paper-wrapped fire is a lantern and a legless chicken is the name of a dish made of bean curd. Do you understand now?'

Both girls were delighted with Fung Ku's advice and after thanking her profusely they went their separate ways. Fifteen days later, as Chang Ku Lao had requested, the girls returned home carrying their appropriate presents. Chang Ku Lao was impressed by their quick wits and decided that he had underestimated their intelligence. But the two girls did not hide the truth: they told their father-in-law about their meeting with the pork butcher's daughter.

'If everything you say is true she must be a very intelligent woman. She sounds as though she would make an ideal daughter-in-law,' exclaimed Chang Ku Lao.

Early the next morning Chang Ku Lao visited the pork butcher but the man had left for market and Fung Ku was alone in the house.

'Good morning, sir. How can I help you?' inquired Fung Ku.

'I want one pound of skin leaning against skin and one pound of skin hitting skin,' replied Chang Ku Lao.

Without hesitation Fung Ku disappeared into the dark storeroom at the back of the shop.

She returned quickly and handed Chang Ku Lao two parcels wrapped in lotus leaves which he unwrapped in front of her. One parcel contained pigs' ears and the other contained pigs' tails. Once again she had solved Chang Ku Lao's riddle correctly and he was delighted at her intelligence. This is the woman I need as a daughter-in-law, he thought to himself. She's the only one who can bring any sense into my house.

Chang Ku Lao returned home and offered prayers to the gods; then he summoned the matchmaker. By the autumn, when both couples had approved the match, marriage contracts were drawn up by the village master and a sumptuous wedding feast was held in Chang Ku Lao's home. Fung Ku proved to be a meticulous and efficient housewife and through her good influence everyone under Chang Ku Lao's roof lived together in harmony.

P'an Ku's Creation

At the beginning of time there was an egg of inconceivable size filled with darkness and chaos. Inside the egg, P'an Ku, the ancestor of all humans, was conceived from chaos. Fed by the darkness, he slowly grew amid the formless mass and for eighteen thousand years he was unaware of any life outside his black cocoon.

One day a sudden movement jolted him awake, but it was too dark to see anything and his initial fear was soon replaced by anger at being trapped. He raced through the chaos lashing out with his fists and eventually smashed the hard black shell surrounding him. Immediately the clarity and light that had been obscured for so long poured out of the egg and rose to the sky and everything that was muddy and dark fell to the earth. From that time the heavens and the earth were clearly divided. But P'an Ku could not be sure that the light and the dark would not collapse into the chaos from whence they originally came, and so he supported the heavens with his head and held the earth firmly in place with his feet.

As each year passed the heavens and the earth grew

farther apart and P'an Ku's body stretched to accommodate them. At the end of eighteen thousand years the top of the heavens and the bottom of the earth could no longer be seen, but P'an Ku tirelessly held them apart in case chaos should ever return. Thousands of years passed and everything that was clear and light became firmly established in the sky and all things muddy and dark settled in the earth.

Secure in the knowledge that the world was safe, P'an Ku collapsed from exhaustion and began to die. His final breath became the wind and the clouds, his voice turned into thunder, his left eye flew to the heavens to become the sun and his right eye swiftly followed to become the moon. P'an Ku's lifeless torso and limbs became flat plains and rocky mountains, his blood flowed swiftly as streams and rivers, his tendons turned into roads and paths and his muscles changed into soil. His thick grey hair and long beard became the stars, his skin and fine body hair fell to earth and took root as grass, trees and flowers, and his teeth, bones and marrow changed into minerals, rubies and jade. Even the sweat on his body fell as rain and dew. He offered his body to the world and when he died he also gave birth to all life.

The Emperor's Commands

Chu Yuan Ch'ang was orphaned just after his birth and unwillingly adopted by a distant uncle. At the age of two Chu Yuan Ch'ang contracted a skin disease on his scalp and not even the most experienced herbalists could heal his scabs and swollen sores. He was known to everyone, even to his uncle, as Swollen-Headed Ch'ang and he had a reputation for being a lazy, gluttonous boy.

One afternoon, while his uncle was tilling one of his fields to plant maize, Chu Yuan Ch'ang seized the opportunity to play in a nearby peanut field. At that time peanuts always grew above the ground, so whenever the boy was hungry he only had to kneel down and eat as many nuts as he wanted. Chu Yuan Ch'ang passed a carefree afternoon eating nuts, climbing trees and chasing any rabbits which ventured into the peanut field. Too many peanuts and too much exercise made him feel drowsy, so he lay down to sleep on the rough peanut stalks in the middle of the field. He dozed fitfully for about an hour but the sharp stalks dug so painfully into his scalp they made sleep impossible.

He stood up, ripped the plants from the soil and stamped angrily on them.

'You stupid peanuts, I hate you. Why don't you grow underneath the ground, not on top of it?'

To his amazement the peanuts began to move across the soil. At first they moved slowly, creeping over one another and intertwining their stems, then they were over-come by a rush of energy and began to burrow feverishly into the soil. Soon they had disappeared from view and the surface of the field looked as though it had been freshly ploughed.

Although Swollen-Headed Ch'ang didn't realize it from that day every peanut grew beneath the soil. At first the farmers were bewildered when their peanuts failed to grow above ground, but they gradually came to accept this change as a decree from Heaven. Nobody realized the power of Chu Yuan Ch'ang's words, least of all the boy himself.

Several months after the mysterious event in the peanut field Chu Yuan Ch'ang was put in charge of his uncle's geese. Swollen-Headed Ch'ang took the geese to the river in the morning, lay on the river bank all day and drove the geese home in the evening.

One day, when the noon heat was too much to bear, Chu Yuan Ch'ang took off his clothes for a cooling swim. Below him in the crystal clear water he saw a purple fish swimming slowly along the river bed. With the speed of lightning Chu Yuan Ch'ang dived into the water and caught the fish with his bare hands. The fish struggled in the young boy's firm grip but it died soon after leaving the water. Using twigs Chu Yuan Ch'ang built a small fire and roasted the fish on a spit made from the branch of a tree. When it was cooked Swollen-Headed Ch'ang reclined against a thick tree trunk and began to eat the fish with his bare hands. He ate slowly so as to relish every bite but he was only halfway through his delicious meal when he heard his uncle approaching. As the boy regretfully tossed the half-eaten fish back into the water he called out to it, 'My sweet-tasting fish, come back to life so that I can eat you again one day.'

The half-eaten fish dutifully came back to life. One half of its body was purple and the other half, the half which had been eaten, was white. Ch'ang had pushed one of the fish's eyes across its head so that both eyes were now on the purple side of its body. The fish survived and bred and became known as a sole by the people who caught it.

Several weeks later, when Ch'ang was guarding his uncle's geese, a group of friends arrived to celebrate the Autumn Moon Festival. They had bowls of rice but no meat, so they asked him to kill a goose and cook it over an open fire.

'Of course I will,' replied Ch'ang eagerly. 'No problem at all. In fact I will kill all the geese and we can eat and eat until we are unable to move.'

Ch'ang swiftly broke the neck of every goose and his friends plucked the carcasses while he prepared a spit over an open fire. The boys passed the afternoon eating, laughing and singing and at dusk they each returned to their own homes leaving Ch'ang alone on the hillside.

It was only then that Ch'ang realized what he had done and he vowed to Heaven not to return until he had found a flock of geese to replace the one he had killed, no matter how long that might take.

Once again the fortune of Heaven shone on him and a flock of white swans flew overhead. Ch'ang called out to them, 'Swans, swans, fly down to me and I will make your leader King of the Swans.'

Miraculously the swans lowered their elegant necks and dived gracefully towards the earth, landing within inches of Ch'ang's feet. He joyously led them home and locked them in a wooden corral for the night.

As usual Ch'ang ate his dinner, then dozed contentedly in front of a log fire while his uncle checked everything in the farmyard before retiring for the night. Ch'ang was awoken by his uncle summoning him to the farmyard.

'What foolish games have you been playing? Why are my geese white? And look at their necks! Why are they twice as long as before?'

Swollen-Headed Ch'ang looked innocently at his uncle and replied, 'This morning, when I led the geese to the hillside, a strong southerly wind and a storm of hail whipped through the valleys and over the hills. The wind stretched their necks and the hail turned their feathers white.'

His uncle considered this explanation for a while but could not think of a better reason for this sudden change, so he let Ch'ang go back to sleep.

The following day Ch'ang's uncle called him early in the morning but Ch'ang rolled over in bed and fell asleep again. His uncle called him twice more during the morning but both times Ch'ang ignored him. At noon Ch'ang's uncle stormed into the bedroom, grabbed him by the scruff of his nightshirt and pulled him out of bed and hit him across his swollen head.

'Leave me alone, you old fool,' shouted Ch'ang. 'Today is Flying Goose Day and unless you keep the gate locked they will fly away. Why should I leave my warm bed to stand by a gate all day?'

'Do you take me for an idiot?' demanded his uncle. 'I have been caring for geese all my life and I've never heard such a lame excuse. Get out of bed this moment before I kick you senseless and take the geese to the mountainside.'

Ch'ang grudgingly pulled on his clothes, trudged into the farmyard and opened the gate of the corral. There was a flurry of feathers and the geese jostled with one another to escape. As soon as they were clear of the gates they ran in an ungainly fashion over the ground, soared gracefully into the air and disappeared for ever over the hill behind the cottage.

This was the final straw for Ch'ang's exasperated uncle.

He threw Ch'ang out of the house and forbade him ever to return. That night Ch'ang slept on a bed of dry leaves in the forest, protected by a worn cotton blanket, his only possession.

For months on end Ch'ang travelled across the country, usually begging food from hospitable farmers and villagers he met on his way. He preferred to live on charity and only worked if he was starving. Ever since he had been banned from his uncle's house he had lost his power of command, and even though he was too lazy to make his own living he knew in his heart that good fortune lay ahead of him. He had convinced himself that it was only a matter of time.

Ch'ang frequently encountered skirmishes between government troops and rebels along his journeys but at the least sign of trouble he would hide himself in the nearest barn, wood or ditch. The Yuan dynasty was drawing to a close and the country was on the verge of civil war. There was even a rumour that the new Emperor, the Son of Heaven, had already been born and was waiting for an opportune moment to take command.

At that time an astrologer, Liu Po Wen, took it upon himself to find the Son of Heaven. He led an assorted band of forest outlaws, all determined to find and crown the new Emperor even if it meant fighting to the death. One day, Liu Po Wen and his outlaws arrived at a wooden bridge and spotted a swollen-headed youth spreadeagled across a boat, asleep. An umbrella shielded the boy's head from the bitter wind. The outlaws were astounded at this sight for the boy's shape formed the Chinese character for 'Emperor'. They shouted to him from the bridge but Ch'ang merely grumbled, turned his back on them and pulled his umbrella down over his head so that his new shape formed the Chinese character for 'Son'. The outlaws could not believe their good fortune and scrambled feverishly down the river bank in case the boy should escape.

Liu Po Wen proclaimed Ch'ang the Son of Heaven and the outlaws led the swollen-headed boy through the villages and towns, heralding him as the founder of the new dynasty. Everyone who heard the astrologer's proclamation acknowledged his superior wisdom and bowed low in front of the aspiring Emperor. Liu Po Wen's prediction was correct. Swollen-headed Chu Yuan Ch'ang eventually became the first Emperor of the Ming dynasty.

The Donkey's Powers

Many years ago in ancient China an honest silk merchant led his donkey into the town of Ch'ien Chou, which was built on the floor of a steep, secluded valley. He arrived in the evening as the local people were taking an evening stroll and dining on *dim sum* in the many small restaurants. As the merchant led his donkey through the main street the startled townsfolk rose from their tables in disbelief, for they had never seen a donkey before. Some of the children were delighted to see this strange monster and some were petrified by its rough grey coat and its piercing bray. The more excited the townsfolk became the louder the donkey brayed and bared its teeth. Delighted to receive so much unexpected attention, the donkey trotted through the streets with a new confidence while the merchant walked happily behind him.

That night the donkey tossed and turned but he could not fall asleep. He eventually decided to exhaust himself by galloping through the night. He ran and ran but failed to notice where he was going, so when he finally stopped he was lost in the forest. He decided to lie down and wait for daybreak.

He was awakened by the cold dew on his nose and in his ears, and a shiver ran down his back when he noticed his damp coat. He stood up, shook himself and lowered his head to eat some grass before heading off in search of the village. While he ate he heard something whispering behind him. Gradually the whispers turned into a loud chattering noise, so loud he was unable to concentrate on his breakfast. When he looked round he saw a row of inquisitive spectators fascinated by his strange shape and huge size.

If the townsfolk were so surprised at me, I imagine these animals can't believe their eyes. I'll give them something to think about, he said to himself.

The donkey raised his head, let out a deafening hee-haw and kicked his rear legs in the air. The animals gave a petrified screech and dashed for cover in their nests and lairs. Only the parrot was not afraid, and clapped his wings in delight and flew swiftly to the tiger to tell him what he had seen. Meanwhile the donkey, extremely pleased with his show of strength, continued with his breakfast.

On hearing the parrot's story, the tiger was keen to meet this potential rival. He rushed through the undergrowth to have a look at the strange beast. Not far from the clearing he stopped to collect his thoughts and then gingerly approached the spot where the donkey was still eating. He was filled with despair when he saw how big the donkey was and decided that he must test his adversary's skill to see if his own supremacy was seriously challenged.

The naive donkey spotted the tiger from the corner of his eye but, never having seen a tiger before, he saw no reason to be afraid of him and decided to give the tiger a hint of his strength by grinding his teeth as loudly as he could.

The tiger recoiled into the undergrowth in horror, afraid that the donkey might eat him if the noise of his teeth was a measure of their sharpness. The donkey was enjoying his newfound celebrity so much that he let out a fearsome hissing sound from between his teeth. But the tiger had accidentally slipped into a muddy ditch and failed to hear the noise. Unfortunately the forest animals had seen his inglorious fall and the King of the Jungle emerged from the ditch wet, dirty and embarrassed.

The donkey watched the tiger approach and crouch down a few feet away from him. By now the donkey felt as though he could fight and beat the animals of the forest singlehandedly. Without a flicker of trepidation he advanced towards the unfortunate tiger, raised his rear legs and kicked him in the shoulder. The tiger was knocked into a thorn bush. He emerged licking his wounds and limping on his left leg but more determined than ever to regain his prowess.

The tiger prowled slowly around the edge of the clearing, mulling over the situation. He noticed that the donkey did not have sharp claws and it seemed to him that his adversary had shown off his only weapons of defence, his hooves and his teeth. The tiger approached the donkey and playfully caught his tail and back legs with his claws. In retaliation the donkey let out a loud bray and kicked his hooves in the air once again.

So I'm right, thought the tiger to himself. All he can do is kick his legs in the air and make a loud noise.

At that the tiger leaped on the unsuspecting donkey and dug his teeth into the animal's neck. The donkey had no chance to escape and no skills to defend himself. While the forest animals looked on in admiration the tiger enjoyed a sumptuous meal of *dim sum*.

The news of the donkey's fate spread rapidly far and wide and ever since then the donkeys have lived on the open plains and hillsides far away from the dangerous forest.

The Sun and Moon Lake

Many years ago thirty families belonging to the Ts'ao clan lived peacefully and prosperously, fishing, hunting and farming the lands of Tai Wan. One autumn morning, while they were harvesting their crops, the sun was hidden by rolling black clouds and the roar of thunder drowned out the shouts of the farmworkers and the barking of dogs. The clouds darkened until the sky turned black and the light of the sun was obliterated.

The villagers huddled together in the fields waiting for the sky to clear, but the hours passed and the day remained as dark as night. The villagers groped their way home in the darkness using trees and fences as landmarks and it was only when the moon rose that they saw each other's faces clearly again. But no sooner had the moon appeared than the thunder began to roll with even more menace than before and the moon disappeared from view.

The people of the Ts'ao tribe no longer saw the sun and moon, and the days and nights were so black that the people could not even see their own fingers. The crops were starved of sunshine and rotted in the fields, the fish swam in the deepest waters and their skin became transparent, the ducks and geese could no longer see where they were flying and refused to eat, so before long they wasted to skin and bone. The birds refused to sing, the flowers did not open their petals, the skin of every villager turned grey and the laughter of children was no longer heard. The village that was once full of happiness was frightened and melancholy.

Six months before this disaster overtook the village, Ta Chien and She Chien had married amid celebrations that lasted two days. They had been given a plot of land on which to grow millet and they relied completely upon the sun for their survival. But since the sun and moon had disappeared they began to fear that they, like many other people in the village, would die of hunger. In desperation they packed two small bags of rice and by the light of a torch they went in search of the sun and the moon. Everywhere they went the starving and the dying were huddled around fires sharing their meagre supplies of food. Strangers stared at them with empty eyes having lost the will to greet them. Even the guard dogs whimpered at their approach, a look of helplessness in their albino-white eyes.

The couple walked until they collapsed with exhaustion and, after sleeping, they pressed on across unknown mountains and plains. Every so often they stumbled over the branches of dead trees and used this wood to light their way. After countless days they approached the arid slopes of Shui She. Just as they reached its craggy peak their torch gave a flicker and died. As they stood clinging to each other for warmth and comfort against the biting wind, She Chien saw a faint patch of light glinting on a lake on the far side of the mountain.

'Look, look over there!' she cried ecstatically, and she broke free from her husband's arms and began to run wildly down the mountain. Her husband followed her, oblivious of the razor-sharp stones that sliced his feet. They ran and slipped, rolled and fell down the steep slopes, but nothing could prevent them from reaching the light upon the lake.

As they drew closer the young couple screamed in delight, for there upon the lake lay the sun and the moon. While they stood laughing and kissing each other they heard a roar from a huge cavern at the side of the lake. In fright, they took refuge behind one of the many enormous boulders dotted around the lakeside. Two fiery dragons emerged from the cavern and lumbered towards the lake. They jumped into its icy waters and headed straight towards the sun and the moon. But instead of extinguishing their radiant light, the dragons lifted the sun and the moon in their scaly paws and with the ease of a juggler they threw them across the lake to each other.

The young couple were outraged to see the sun and the moon being treated with such frivolity, but they were powerless against the force of these mighty creatures.

While Ta Chien and She Chien discussed what they should do, a small twist of smoke came from the boulder they were leaning against. They carefully pushed the boulder to one side and found a deep tunnel cut into the rocky hillside. In the distance, beyond the damp, slimy walls, they saw the warm glow of a fire. Driven on by the hope of retrieving the sun and the moon, they anxiously headed towards its beckoning glow.

The long tunnel ended in a dry, well-swept, stone-lined cavern. In one corner an old woman was stoking the red-hot embers of a stove. Ta Chien and She Chien crept cautiously through the narrow entrance into the cavern, but the old woman heard their footsteps and swung round, brandishing an iron poker at the petrified couple.

'What are you doing here? Don't take a step further until you tell me what you want,' demanded the old woman.

'Please help us,' begged She Chien. 'We haven't come to harm you. We need your help.'

The old woman eyed their torn clothes, their bloody feet and their hollowed faces. She had not seen other humans for many years and had no reason to turn them away. After offering them a place by the stove she gradually revealed how the dragons had forcibly carried her to this cave after she had poured a cauldron of boiling oil into one of the lake's tributaries. The oil had burned the dragons' skin and her punishment was a lifetime in their service. She had lost count of the number of years she had been there, but she had been young when she first arrived and now her skin was gnarled and her fingers bent. As she talked she touched the young couple from time to time to check they were real for she had been sure she would die without ever seeing humans again.

When the old woman had finished speaking the young couple told her about the disaster that had befallen the land during her years of captivity and of their long search for the sun and the moon. The old woman listened with admiration to their courageous tale but her heart was heavy when she heard of life beyond the confines of the cave. Eventually all three sat silently not knowing where to go or what to do. The old woman broke the silence. 'I know what we can do. I know how to kill the dragons. I have heard tales of a golden axe and scissors buried beneath Li Shan Mountain. It's not far from here. They are the only things in the world that the dragons are afraid of. If you drop the scissors and the axe into the lake the axe will chop the dragons' heads off and the scissors will cut them into tiny pieces. Then and only then will you be able to retrieve the sun and the moon.'

Ta Chien and She Chien were not daunted by the task ahead of them. After sharing a meal with the old woman the young couple armed themselves with two cast-iron shovels and set off for Li Shan. Following the old woman's directions, they soon reached the mountain.

They immediately began to dig and continued to dig until their hands were torn and blistered and their backs ached so that they could no longer move. When they were too tired to dig any longer they fell asleep, but the moment they awoke they started again regardless of pangs of hunger in their stomachs, the pain in their limbs or their swollen hands. Again they dug until they dropped from exhaustion, slept until their strength was renewed and then continued determinedly with their search.

After days of fruitless searching their shovels jarred against metal objects in the earth. Ta Chien and She Chien scrabbled in the soil digging out the golden axe and scissors with their hands. Finally they held the precious objects in their arms and headed back to the dragons' lake. Careful not to stumble on the sharp rocks and lose their priceless find on the mountainside, they crept cautiously onto a narrow ledge overhanging the lake. She Chien lifted the axe above her head and threw it with all her might at the dragons juggling the sun and moon in the lake. But instead of flying downwards the axe flew upwards, hung in the air for several moments, then, followed by a streak of lightning, dived towards the dragons. Before they knew what was happening the dragons' heads had been sliced off with one clean cut. A fountain of blood, higher than the mountains themselves, gushed into the air.

Ta Chien raised the scissors into the air and hurled them into the blood-red water. The scissors took on a life of their own and charged through the water slashing the dragons' limbs, bodies and heads. Soon pieces of the hacked bodies were strewn across the mountainside or sank to the bottom of the lake. Suddenly everything was peaceful and calm. Nothing moved except the sun and moon, which bobbed gently on the lake.

Without losing a moment Ta Chien and She Chien ran back to the cavern to free the old woman. Then all three returned to the lake for there was still work to be done. They retrieved the sun and the moon but they did not have the strength to replace them in the sky. Once again the old woman recalled a tale she had heard in her youth many years ago.

'They say that you will be given supernatural powers if you eat the eyes of a dragon. Perhaps you will be filled with enough strength to put the sun back in the sky.'

Ta Chien and She Chien had seen and heard so many strange things on their travels that they were willing to eat the dragons' eyes, if only they could find them. Guided by the light from the sun and the moon, they searched the mountainside for the heads. They found one head wedged between the rocks on the lakeside. They ripped out the eyes and swallowed one each.

As the eyes dissolved in their stomachs they were charged with tremendous strength. At first their feet began to grow, then they felt their legs being stretched, next their bodies and finally their necks and heads. They grew and grew, until they were taller than the highest mountain. They stooped down and gently lifted the sun and moon into the sky.

But the sun and moon had forgotten how to stay in space and as soon as Ta Chien and She Chien let go of them they came tumbling back to earth with a mighty crash.

Once again the old woman came to their help. 'Why don't you set them on the strong branches of those tall pine trees and replant the pine trees on the highest peak? The sun and moon can rest there until they remember their old home and are no longer afraid to float.'

Ta Chien and She Chien were able to uproot two of the tallest pine trees and replant them without any difficulty, but the powerful effect of the dragon's eyes was beginning to wear off. The sun and moon were safe but the young couple had shrunk to their normal size.

All three waited anxiously by the lakeside for something to happen but nothing moved and after several anxious hours they burned offerings to the gods and said prayers to Heaven. As the smoke drifted towards the sky the sun and moon rose from the pine trees. They rose higher and higher until, once more, they were in their correct positions in the heavens.

The young couple and the old woman rejoiced as they watched the moon sink behind the horizon and the sun shine across the whole country. The sun in time sank behind the horizon and the moon took its place. Once again the crops began to grow, the animals began to multiply and the people grew healthy.

The old woman returned to her family, but Ta Chien and She Chien were afraid to leave the lake for fear that other dragons might decide to steal the sun and the moon. They stayed so long that they took root in the earth, and at their death a wild hurricane struck the lake and their bodies changed into mountains. Ta Chien Mountain and She Chien Mountain can be seen to this day and each year villagers gather at the lakeside to take part in the Sun and Moon Dance in memory of them.

Wang Erh and the Golden Hairpin

Wang Erh, the woodcutter, lived in a small wooden hut on the edge of a dense forest which lay a day's walk from the palace of the Emperor. One noon, while he was chopping wood in a forest clearing, a dense black cloud passed overhead blocking out the sun. Wang Erh looked long and hard at the cloud and could discern the shape of a man; in its thick mists he caught a glimpse of a young girl frantically waving her hands. It was only then that it dawned on Wang Erh that the girl was being kidnapped, not by a man but by a devil. He picked up his axe, ran after the cloud and as soon as he was in aiming distance he hurled the axe into the mists. The swirling cloud obscured his view but he heard a piercing cry and, a few moments later, saw a trickle of blood upon the ground. It marked a trail on the forest floor as the cloud moved slowly on.

Wang Erh followed the bloody track through the forest until he reached a faraway valley. It was nightfall. The cloud stopped halfway up the valley side and disappeared without trace. As he scrambled up the hill by the light of the moon Wang Erh unexpectedly came across a cave, hollowed into the hillside, just below the spot where the cloud had disappeared. Cautiously he crept inside, but although he could hear mumblings and mutterings echoing from deep underground, it was too dark to see anything. Uncertain what to do, he crept stealthily out of the cave and returned home.

That night Wang Erh racked his brains. He devised many plans and eventually came up with what appeared to be a foolproof scheme. Delighted with his new idea, Wang Erh went to the local market shortly after dawn to enlist the help of friends working on the marketstalls. When he arrived there was pandemonium in the marketplace with the villagers gossiping avidly to one another and a detachment of the Emperor's guards marching round questioning everyone who crossed their path.

'What is it? What's happened?' demanded Wang Erh of a passing farmer.

'Haven't you heard?' answered the farmer incredulously, 'The Emperor's only daughter was kidnapped by a monstrous devil yesterday morning and nobody has seen or heard of her since. The Emperor is offering his daughter's hand in marriage to the man who rescues her. Just think, the Emperor's daughter could marry any one of us.'

With that the farmer ran off excitedly to find out exactly where the princess had been kidnapped so that he could begin his search.

Eventually the previous day's events became clear to Wang Erh and he rushed to the palace and demanded an audience with the Emperor.

The Emperor was willing to see anyone who had news of his daughter and he had already spent half the night listening to tales from fools and fortune hunters trying to convince him that they knew her whereabouts. Wang Erh was eventually summoned to the audience hall and, after bowing low before the Emperor, he began his story. At first the Emperor listened distractedly but as the tale unfolded he sat up with interest. Wang Erh's story seemed extremely plausible and, furthermore, the young woodcutter was able to describe the princess's appearance in enough detail to convince the Emperor that what he said was true.

Wang Erh sensed the Emperor's interest and he finished his account by asking for 500 pigs, an axe, a large basket, a bell and a rope measuring 1000 feet in length. The Emperor not only gave Wang Erh what he had requested but also ordered one of his captains and a band of twenty soldiers to accompany the woodcutter on his mission.

After two days' march the expedition arrived at the cave and cautiously followed Wang Erh into its gloomy interior. By the light of a single torch they tied a pig to the end of a rope and lowered it down a deep shaft which they found in the corner of the cave. Everybody waited silently as the pig was lowered deeper and deeper into the hillside. As soon as it reached the bottom they heard a scurrying of feet and muffled squeals of delight rose from the depths. The captain of the guard hauled up the rope. The pig had gone but the end of the rope was torn and bloody. Another 499 pigs were lowered down the shaft and each time the rope returned in the same state.

After the last pig had been lowered Wang Erh tied the bell to the basket and then, clasping the axe, squeezed himself inside. Under orders from Wang Erh to raise the basket when the bell rang, three soldiers lowered the woodcutter slowly down the shaft.

After what seemed an interminable journey, Wang Erh landed in a huge cavern dimly lit by a fire. As his eyes became accustomed to the darkness, he saw, slumped on the floor around him, a large number of devils. Some were snoring loudly, others were groaning with pain or delight as they rubbed their extended stomachs. They failed to notice this stranger in their midst and so, clutching his axe, Wang Erh cautiously climbed out of the basket.

Stealthily, he stopped by every devil and sliced off its head with one fell of his finely honed axe. Before long the cave was a mass of rolling heads and bloody corpses.

In the silence of the cavern he heard a faint cry which seemed to echo round the thick mossy walls. Wang Erh headed in the direction of the sound and found himself facing a low, roughly hewn passageway hollowed out of the cavern wall.

He crept along the dirty, dank passageway on his hands and knees and before long reached another large, gloomy chamber. In the centre he saw the princess. She was leaning against a washing tub full of clothes and weeping. Wang Erh called gently to her so as not to disturb any other devils that might be lurking in the shadows. The princess looked up in amazement as Wang Erh slowly approached. He bowed low before her.

'I can hardly believe my eyes! Who are you? How did you find me? How do you know who I am?' she cried out.

Wang Erh quickly explained the events of the past three days but did not waste time with details. 'You can ask me as many questions as you like when you are free, but what I need to know now is where the king of the devils is hiding?'

'He's resting in his cave. He was so badly wounded by your axe that he can't walk, and I'm meant to tend his wounds.'

The princess pointed to a narrow corridor in the far corner of the cavern which led to a cave where the king of the devils lay semiconscious. Following Wang Erh's instructions, the princess prepared a hot poultice to put on the devil's head, and then she crept along the tunnel, closely followed by Wang Erh. The devil lay in a delirious state on his bed, clutching his head and moaning quietly.

'My devil king, I have something to ease your pain,' said the princess soothingly. 'Just close your eyes and relax. I will soon make you better.'

While she gently laid the poultice on the devil's forehead, Wang Erh crept up behind him and slashed the devil across the back of his skull. The force of the blow cracked his skull in two, killing him instantly.

Wang Erh led the princess back through the low passageways and caverns to the basket in which the soldiers had lowered him into the cave. He lifted the princess inside, rang the bell three times, and soon the soldiers were hauling her to the surface. Before she disappeared from Wang Erh's sight, she pulled a golden hairpin from her thick black hair, snapped it into two pieces and threw one piece to her rescuer.

'Thank you for saving me, Wang Erh. Keep this pin as a memento, and if you need to find me use it to prove who you are. Come to the palace . . .'

But her words faded as she was hauled closer to daylight and to safety, leaving Wang Erh alone in the darkness with the devils. He waited patiently for the basket to be lowered but nothing happened. He could see a speck of daylight way above his head and he shouted to the soldiers, but there was no reply. For fear of attracting more devils Wang Erh ceased his cries for help and waited patiently in the cavern, his eyes transfixed on the circle of daylight.

At first he thought that night had fallen unexpectedly or that his eyes were playing tricks, but then it slowly dawned on him that the soldiers were filling the entrance with huge boulders, blocking his only route of escape.

Meanwhile the princess had been taken immediately to the palace. After she had gone the captain of the guard ordered his soldiers to seal off the cave and, under the threat of death, not to reveal what had happened.

On returning to the palace the captain related to the Emperor how Wang Erh had bravely tried to rescue the princess but had been eaten by the devils the moment he stepped foot in the cavern. Undeterred, he himself had climbed down into the dangerous hole and had single-handedly murdered more than a hundred devils to rescue the princess. The Emperor was accordingly impressed by this heroic account and offered the cunning captain the promised reward, his daughter's hand in marriage.

The princess was heartbroken when she heard the news and demanded that the captain prove his story. But her pleas fell on deaf ears for the Emperor had already given his word and set a wedding date. Soon the news was officially announced in every province and preparations for local and national celebrations were begun. While the palace officials and local governors were excitedly holding meetings and making plans, the princess slowly wasted away in her room, refusing to eat or to speak. Every day the herbalist invented new remedies for her sickness but none had the desired effect. She could only utter two words, 'Wang Erh', again and again.

After the entrance to the cavern had been sealed Wang Erh paced the subterranean passageways desperately trying to find an escape route. It seemed to him that many hours and possibly even days had passed since the princess had been rescued and there was little chance that he would ever see her again. He returned regularly to the spot where the basket had been lowered hoping to see rescuers in the small opening overhead but he could not even make out the roof in the darkness.

Eventually Wang Erh heard yelps and shufflings from a nearby cavern and he hastily fumbled his way to a low dark room as far away from the sounds as possible. He had not discovered this room before and was surprised to hear a gentle gurgling noise very close to where he was standing. As he edged his way towards the noise he tripped over a wickerwork basket lying on the floor. Wang Erh stooped to pick up the basket and peered inside. A yellow light stunned him for a moment. It was shining from a golden carp. He reached out to touch it to make sure it was not a vision or a devil's trick. The carp responded to his gentle touch with a flap of its tail. Its beautiful smooth head had been pinned to the basket by a rusty iron nail. Pained by the sight of the suffering fish, Wang Erh pulled the nail out of its golden body. As soon as the nail had been drawn out of the flesh the basket was thrown into the air by a powerful force and at that instant a handsome youth stood before Wang Erh. The boy bowed low in gratitude and said, 'May the gods of Heaven bless you for saving my life. I'm a prince of the sea, third son of the Sea Dragon King. Two days ago I was travelling down a nearby river when I was ambushed by the devils of this cavern. I imagined I would never feel the waters on my skin again but you have rescued me and it's my duty to repay you.'

The prince produced three pills and a carved shell from the pocket of his silk brocade jacket. He gave Wang Erh the shell and two of the pills.

'Trust me,' said the prince. 'I'm going to swallow one of these pills and you must do the same. Your only escape is through the underground river that flows through this cavern. The other pill you can use whenever you are in need. Now swallow one pill immediately.'

Wang Erh obeyed the prince and felt his body change into a streamlined silver carp. As he slid into the river behind the prince he heard frantic yells and screams echoing through the nearby corridors. They swam silently upstream through the dark waters until Wang Erh felt the warmth of the sun strike his silver body and knew that he had finally escaped. With a flick of his tail he jumped onto the river bank. As a gesture of farewell the prince leaped into the air then dived back into the fast-flowing waters.

Wang Erh crawled to a dry spot on the river bank and fell into a deep sleep. When he awoke at dawn he had changed back into a man, but the dry fish scales on his skin reassured him that the previous night's events were real. He washed himself in the river, picked some fruit from a nearby tree and made his way as quickly as possible to the palace, spurred on by talk in every village he passed through of the forthcoming marriage of the princess. When he arrived at the palace gates the Emperor's guards doubted his story, but took pity on him nevertheless and permitted him access to an audience with the Emperor.

Wang Erh prostrated himself before the Emperor and lay the carved shell upon a silk brocade footstool at the Emperor's feet.

'Your Majesty, you have been tricked. I am the man who saved your daughter. It was I who went into the cave. I killed the devils and risked my life. The captain tried to murder me. Summon the princess and she will prove my story.'

'My daughter is ill, she cannot come. It is up to you to prove your story. What evidence do you have?' demanded the Emperor.

Wang Erh produced the golden hairpin given him by the princess and the Emperor's personal guard presented it to the nurse who in turn laid it on the princess's pillow. As soon as she caught sight of it she sat up.

'It's from him!' she cried. 'It's from the man who saved me.'

To the astonishment of her nurse and her maidservants she left her bed, hastily pulled on a court dress and, although weak from her illness, ran to her father and begged him to believe Wang Erh's story.

The sheer joy of seeing his daughter walk again was enough to convince the Emperor. Before the assembled courtiers he decreed Wang Erh his future son-in-law and publicly denounced the treacherous captain.

Overjoyed with his good fortune, Wang Erh gave his future wife the gift of health in the form of the pill he had received from the sea prince. Now that the princess had recovered her health the whole kingdom made plans to celebrate the wedding with greater excitement than before. And that night, under cover of darkness, a detachment of the king's bravest soldiers were sent to the cavern to destroy every devil and seal the entrance for ever.

The Wild Cat's Mistake

The wild cat who lived on Pa Chien Mountain in Tai Wan was a vain, proud creature. He was covered in sleek golden hair which shimmered in the sunlight. He was well aware of his beauty and had little time for his mountain neighbours. The scaly anteater, on the other hand, was slow and ugly but he was thoughtful, modest and considerate. His back was layered with hard triangular scales and he liked nothing better than extending his long sticky tongue with the speed of lightning and lapping up any ants that crossed his path.

One day the cunning wild cat spotted the scaly anteater sleeping soundly beneath the shade of a banyan tree. The scheming cat climbed stealthily into the banyan tree's branches, gripped the bark as tightly as he could and shook the tree until the noise of cracking branches awoke the scaly anteater from his deep sleep. The scaly anteater was unperturbed and merely moved his position, but the cat continued to shake the tree until an ants' nest was dislodged from the trunk and fell to the ground with a thud. The scaly anteater could not believe his good fortune and fell upon the ant hill with a voracious appetite. The wild cat was furious with himself for providing the anteater with an easy meal and swiftly leaped from the branches and angrily kicked the ants' nest into the dry grass nearby.

'If you expect to eat those ants you must first pay homage to me as the wild cat king,' demanded the wild cat.

But the scaly anteater did not hear him; he had already lumbered off in the direction of the ant hill muttering how kind Heaven had been to bestow such a rich and easy dinner.

By now the wild cat was furious and he bounded towards the dry grass. He crouched between the long stalks until the scaly anteater had settled down to eat his prey and then he set fire to the grass. Within two minutes the whole area was ablaze and the air was full of acrid smoke.

'Enjoy yourself, my friend, because you'll soon make a good roast dinner,' said the wild cat. 'Thank you for the compliment,' replied a voice behind him.

The startled wild cat spun round to see the anteater sitting contentedly on the grass beside him.

'And may I also say thank you for that delicious dinner and that wonderful experience. There is nothing more pleasant than watching bright golden flames leaping up towards a blue sky. You should try it yourself some time.'

'But . . . but you're alive,' stuttered the cat. 'Why didn't you burn? Doesn't the fire hurt? Can I try it?'

'Calm down, wild cat,' replied the scaly anteater. 'I will answer all your questions if you give me a moment. The fire isn't harmful – in fact it's very pleasant and I recommend that you try it. It's an experience that you will never forget. Why don't you enter the fire? There are plenty of roasted snakes and frogs waiting for you in there.'

The thought of food readily available made the greedy wild cat slaver and with a powerful leap he bounced into the middle of the blazing grass. A piercing scream immediately rose from the flames and the cat emerged from the fire running for his life. His fine golden coat had been singed to a dull grey colour. The wily anteater had dug a tunnel in the earth to protect himself and his scales had kept out the fierce heat, but the wild cat's fur offered no such protection.

The wild cat slunk into the shadows to clean his charred fur but he never managed to regain his glorious golden colour. And to this day wild cats keep their dull grey hair hidden from view.

Liang Yu Ching's Punishment

The Jade Emperor built a palace of gold and jade to protect his daughters from the day-to-day life of Heaven as well as from the many immortals and ghosts who made frequent heavenly visits. Everyone, including the maids and the weaving girls, was given permission to wear a star crown so that the palace looked like a revolving heavenly galaxy.

The weaving girls were expected to work harder than anyone else to provide ornate silk gowns for the princesses. It was considered an honour to live in the palace and they were expected to work accordingly. All except two girls fulfilled this duty. Liang Yu Ching and Wei Shing Jwan spent every afternoon catching butterflies and making secret plans to escape to the earth so that they could play whenever and wherever they wanted.

One day the T'ai Pei Star Fairy flew low over the palace garden in her chariot and spotted the two girls huddled in conversation. Bored by her travels and anxious to learn their secrets, she hovered in a cloud above the garden, but the bright light of her star crown startled the weaving girls, who recognized the goddess immediately.

'Come and join us,' cried Liang Yu Ching, 'No one will ever know you're here.'

Without further encouragement the T'ai Pei Star Fairy lowered her chariot to the ground but as soon as its wheels touched the earth the two girls jumped in.

'We have a better idea,' said Wei Shing Jwan. 'Let's play on earth. No one will ever find us there.'

The T'ai Pei Star Fairy was easily persuaded to go to earth for, like the weaving girls, she was only too happy to escape the Jade Emperor's domain.

They landed at Wei City and settled in a grotto outside the town. There was always the possibility that an immortal might spot them so they emerged only at night to carouse until the sun rose.

Forty-six days after their arrival on earth people throughout China noticed that the T'ai Pei Star had disappeared from the sky and to avoid misfortune they made offerings to the Jade Emperor. Meanwhile the Jade Emperor was furious at T'ai Pei's recklessness and had ordered the Five Mountain Gods to find the star fairy and the girls.

The Five Mountain Gods held endless meetings to decide on a plan of action but with the whole of China below them it was difficult to know where to begin. Their solution was to divide the land into five areas – North, South, East, West and Centre – and each god would send out troops and heavenly spies who would be bound to the earth until they discovered the girls.

As the search parties set out the T'ai Pei Star Fairy and the two weaving girls began their night's adventures. As they passed the Eastern Mountain, Liang Yu Ching leaned out of the chariot to have a look at the villages dotted on its slopes, but she leaned too far and her star crown slipped from her head and tumbled down the steep slopes into the valley far below. Unable to see anything in the darkness, she begged the star fairy to stop the chariot and help her scour the mountain for her lost crown.

The three friends left their chariot on the mountain peak and by the light of the two remaining crowns they crawled along the mountain's steep ridges hoping to find the crown before dawn. As they rounded a sharp bend on the mountainside they unexpectedly came face to face with a detachment of troops belonging to the Eastern Mountain God. They turned on their heels and scrambled back up the mountain to their chariot. They ignored the rocks that ripped their silk dresses and tore their skin but in their haste they had forgotten to remove the star crowns that lit the way for the soldiers who were pursuing them.

The T'ai Pei Star Fairy and Liang Yu Ching managed to jump into the chariot in time, but Wei Shing Jwan stumbled on the stony ground and shouted to the others to leave without her. As the chariot rose into the air she ran to a cave hollowed deep inside the mountain and was never seen again.

Unaware that one of their targets had escaped, the soldiers followed the light from the chariot as it sped through the sky and landed outside the grotto near Wei City. Within minutes the grotto was surrounded and the star fairy and Liang Yu Ching were trapped. They were arrested and promptly escorted to Heaven.

The Jade Emperor sat in judgement on his gold throne as the prisoners were forced to bow in obedience before him, forbidden to utter a word in his presence.

'You, T'ai Pei Star Fairy are a responsible star and should set an example. For eternity you will remain in the same position in the sky and will never move again. And you, Liang Yu Ching, one of my chosen weavers, are banished to the Purple Star where you will be surrounded by endless rice fields. You will strip the husk from every grain of rice until I tell you to stop.'

For thousands of years Liang Yu Ching worked in the paddy fields without complaint until the Jade Emperor felt she had served her punishment and decided to grant her a daughter, Hsui-ku, who would take care of her in her old age.

Hsui-ku had been granted many gifts by the repentant Jade Emperor. She was an expert weaver and a skilled singer and she had a generous nature. She was willing to forgive everyone except her mother. Hsui-ku was eventually married to Ho Pei, the river god, and as a wedding gift the Jade Emperor appointed her Goddess of Rain. Each day she patrolled the sky to see which areas were dry and which areas were flooded. As the years went by and the land flourished the people of China grew to respect and worship her.

Even with all this good fortune Hsui-ku refused to forget the shame her mother had brought upon the family. Each time she approached the grotto outside Wei City where the three friends had lived she withheld the rain, and each time the T'ai Pei Star shone brightly Hsui-ku refused to leave Heaven.

Even today the land around Wei City is arid and it never rains when the T'ai Pei Star is at its brightest, although a strange light can sometimes be seen at night on the Eastern Mountain. Some say it is Wei Shing Jwan trying to catch Hsui-ku's attention so that rain will eventually fall in this area.

The Rats' Wedding

The Wah Chiu family lived in a large house near the Chui Li bridge on Yu Mountain in the time of the Ming dynasty. One New Year's Eve the owner of the house heard squeals of excitement coming from a room that had been locked for many years. He unbolted the rusty lock as quietly as he could and crept into the room to witness an unbelievable sight. In the far corner he saw a huge black rat leading a procession of musicians, servants and a bridal party. Six smaller rats danced behind the large rat, each one playing a miniature musical instrument, and the bridegroom, wearing a black hat with a golden flower in it, rode on a tiny white stallion. On either side he was accompanied by four more rats each riding grey mares. The owner of the house was even more amazed when he saw the bridal chair being carried by eight men each no more than a foot high. At the rear was a tearful old man sitting in a sedan chair carried by two rats. The procession wound its way around the room, oblivious of the owner's presence, and disappeared into a crack in the woodwork at the far end of the room.

The owner returned downstairs but did not say anything to his family for fear that he had imagined everything. The next night he again went up to the room and again saw the rats, who were just beginning their wedding feast. During the next eight days he crept up every night to watch the rats continue with their wedding celebrations, and on the tenth night the room shook as everyone danced to celebrate the arrival of the new moon. During the following ten nights the old man who had been sitting in the sedan chair employed a small emaciated tutor to teach his new son-in-law writing and accounting.

After twenty days of secret visits the owner told his family what he had seen, but nobody believed him, and when he led them up to the room on the twenty-first night the rats and the small humans had disappeared.

Although he made regular visits to the room at the top of the house in the following weeks it was always empty and his family assumed that he had been suffering from feverish hallucinations brought on by New Year celebrations.

Several months later the owner was sitting outside his front door watching his neighbours, chatting and playing mahjong when a Taoist priest passed by. The priest stopped, looked at the house and then announced to the owner, 'Your house has a strong evil spirit and I can help you to exorcise it.'

The priest's words confirmed the owner's worries and so he invited the learned man into his house. Without asking for directions the priest went to the room at the top of the house and removed a long sword encased in coins from his belt. He held the sword aloft and blew at the ceiling. His breath rose and formed a dense cloud. The cloud then parted to reveal a household god who pointed to the corner of the room and then disappeared. No sooner had he gone than the small men who had been in the wedding procession came tumbling from the wall and lay in a confused state on the floor. Before they could come to their senses the priest stabbed each one through the heart with his sword. The servants of the house were summoned to clear away their bodies and scrub their blood from the wooden floorboards.

The owner of the house bowed low before the priest and asked him how he could repay him.

'You know I am a Taoist and I do not need rewards for helping others, but I did summon a household god to help me rid the house of evil spirits and I know that he would like to be thanked with food and wine.'

The owner nodded his head in agreement, but after the priest had left he sat down to consider fully the implications of the priest's answer. This was a strange request since it was normal for a household god to banish evil spirits and it was well known that they never sought reward. Furthermore, a Taoist priest would never ask reward on behalf of another god. The owner therefore decided to ignore the priest's request and leave the household god to fend for himself.

As soon as he had made this decision an angry voice rang through the house. 'I've helped you rid the house of evil spirits and now you're too miserly to thank the god who made it possible. I warn you that I'll never leave your family in peace.'

When he heard these threats the owner knew that the priest had been a devil in disguise, but it was too late to alter the fate that lay in store for his family. From that day on his house was thronged with rats who gnawed through the furniture, ate the family's clothes and ravaged the storeroom. Even though they tried to seal the cupboards and containers, nothing prevented the rats attacking and destroying everything the Wah Chiu family owned. No sooner had the servants swept up the debris than the rats were back in force to cause yet more havoc.

After two weeks of this destruction the family were driven from their home. They journeyed to Kiangsi to visit Chang T'ien Shih, the most learned Taoist priest in

China. Chang T'ien Shih was so intrigued by their story that he and his disciples accompanied the Wah Chiu family to see the rats for themselves. In the family's absence the rats had caused devastation in every room, but when they sensed the presence of a powerful Taoist priest they ran for cover, screeching in fear and falling over one another in their haste to escape.

To counter the rats' curse Chang T'ien Shih drew a bag of charms from his flowing purple robe and asked the owner to place them on top of five poles which were then set up around the house as guardians. Then the learned sage went alone to the room at the top of the house where the marriage had taken place. He placed an inscribed piece of peach wood in front of the gap in the wall where the rats had entered on New Year's Eve and stuck two peach-wood swords into the wooden floor in front of the gap. While he did this he recited a slow monotonous chant. When the ritual was completed he returned to the family and his disciples.

After accepting the hospitality of the Wah Chiu family the Taoists returned to Kiangsi and for the first time in weeks the family slept in peace. But five days later they were again troubled by an acrid smell which filled every room and permeated their clothes with its sickening fumes. The terrified owner feared that the rats had returned and was forced to climb the stairs to the room at the top of the house where the smell was most powerful. He ordered his servants to break down the peach-wood seal in the corner of the room and crawl into the hole. The smell was so intense that some of the servants collapsed before they could enter, but those who managed to crawl into the hole let out cries of delight. Chang T'ien Shih's powerful charms and peach wood had killed every rat and the first rats to be removed were the two largest, the two who had placed a curse on the Wah Chiu household.

From that time on everyone who lives around the Yu Mountain and on the northern and southern sides of the

Yangtzi river leaves marriage gifts of salt and rice in the corners of the house and goes to bed early on New Year's Eve so that the rats are left to marry in peace. And in other areas of China there is a traditional day during the New Year festival when the rats have the free run of the house for the night and as much as they can eat and drink so that the family will be left in peace for the coming year.

The Child of the Mulberry Tree

Three thousand seven hundred years ago, during the Hsia dynasty, there lived an old, unmarried woman who managed a mountain farm without help from friends or neighbours. Before sowing seeds or harvesting the land she made offerings to the Jade Emperor, and before cooking any animals she had killed in the forest she made offerings to her ancestors. Throughout her life this woman had lived in harmony with Heaven and earth.

One night she dreamed that the Jade Emperor descended on a cloud from Heaven and as the cloud settled in front of her, the Jade Emperor spoke. 'You have a good heart and generous spirit and I've noticed that you have never failed to make offerings to Heaven. Your reward is a piece of advice that will save your life. Tomorrow you will see water flowing from the stone mortar in which you pound your rice. As soon as it starts to flow you must run to the east, but you must not look behind you under any circumstances until you reach the next village.'

The old woman had no chance to ask the Jade Emperor

why she must not look back, for he disappeared as soon as he had finished speaking.

When she awoke the next morning she remembered everything that had happened in the dream but she put it out of her mind while she prepared to spend the day gathering rice. In the evening as she sat outside her house pounding the rice in a stone mortar, she saw a trickle of water flowing from the base. And it was only then that she remembered the Jade Emperor's words and ran to warn her neighbours.

'Follow me!' she screamed as she ran from house to house. 'Whatever happens and whatever you hear, do not look back.'

The villagers were too startled by her frantic screams to ask any questions and on seeing the fear in the woman's eyes they were convinced that something terrible was about to happen. They streamed across the fields after her even though there was no sign of danger. Ahead of them the sky was clear and the land peaceful but behind them the water which had started as a trickle had turned into turbulent rapids that whipped in and out of the houses, ripping shrubs and bushes that stood in its way. The water flowed across the farm land and engulfed the village.

By this time the villagers were approaching the neighbouring town and the woman, no longer able to contain her curiosity, turned to see the wall of water closing in on her. She immediately turned back to the east but it was too late. The others had disappeared and the water began to engulf her. Her feet sank into the mud and as the water reached her neck her body changed into wood. She raised her arms and screamed for help but nobody heard her and her arms turned into branches. When the water eventually subsided a mulberry tree stood in the spot where the woman had been.

The tree grew close to a small town which had been built and was owned by a wealthy merchant, Yu Sin Shih.

One of his silk weavers heard from her friends that a mulberry tree had mysteriously appeared outside the town and she set out to find it and to gather mulberry leaves for her silkworms. The day was sunny and windless so when the woman heard a child crying she was certain that it came from within the trunk of the tree. She ran her hands slowly around the stem until she reached a soft spot on the gnarled trunk into which she could reach her hand. Her hand sank deeper and deeper and when it seemed to have reached the centre of the tree she felt the soft flesh of a baby. Very gently she pulled the baby out of the tree. Aware that this was no ordinary child, the silkweaver placed it carefully in the mulberry leaves that she had gathered and set off for home.

As the baby had been discovered in a tree that stood close to the banks of the I river the silkweaver called the child I Yin. She offered this baby to her master, Yu Sin Shih, who ordered his servants to feed and rear the child. The child grew to be intelligent and virtuous, always ready to help those in need.

At that time China was governed by Emperor Chieh Kuei, a callous, violent ruler. Noblemen and peasants alike had been disaffected by Chieh Kuei's policies and decisions and plans for a revolution had been made by a respected leader, Ching Tang. On his travels he had heard of I Yin's courageous, noble character and after their first meeting he asked I Yin to join him. I Yin refused twice, but at the third request he finally agreed to join Ching Tang. After years of careful planning they staged the revolution and, with the help of sympathetic noblemen close to the Emperor, Chieh Kuei was finally overthrown.

Ching Tang established the Shang dynasty and appointed I Yin Prime Minister. The man who was conceived by flood waters and born from a mulberry tree governed as Prime Minister for more than a hundred years.

Kuan Yin

The 19th day of the 6th month of the lunar calendar is the anniversary of Kuan Yin's ascension to heaven as a Bodhisattva. She is the Goddess of Sympathy and Mercy and is worshipped by Chinese Buddhists throughout the world. But Kuan Yin was not always a goddess and this story tells how she attained the state of Bodhisattva.

Long before historical records were kept there was a small nation called Hsing Lin ruled by a king who had three daughters. The youngest daughter, Maio Shan, was the most intelligent, generous and beautiful of the three sisters. Her thoughts and actions were always directed to those in need and tales of her kindness were soon known by the courtiers and servants of the palace.

One evening, while she was sitting under a pine tree in the palace gardens, she heard a cicada chattering above her head. Gradually its drowsy sound lulled her to sleep. Suddenly, she was jolted out of her dreams by the screaming of the cicada. She jumped up and saw a praying mantis with its powerful legs encircling the cicada's body. Maio Shan jumped onto a stone bench to release the cicada from the praying mantis's grasp. In anger the praying mantis swiftly turned to attack the young girl's fingers. She withdrew her hand, lost her balance and fell onto the paved path beside the stone bench. She was shaken but conscious and when she stood up a stream of blood ran from a deep cut on her forehead. When her sisters found her and consoled her she shrugged her shoulders and replied, 'A scar on my forehead is a small price to pay for the life of a cicada.'

When the gash on her forehead healed it formed a scar and over the years the scar turned into a patch of red moles, which is why statues and pictures of Kuan Yin always show her with moles on her face.

Maio Shan was considerate to humans as well. She could not bear to see others suffer and when her mother died after a prolonged illness she was inconsolable. Again and again she asked the heavenly beings why humans should suffer so much and what she could do to help them. One morning as she repeated these requests in front of a statue of the Buddha the temple was filled with a golden light and the statue came to life.

'My good child,' the statue said, 'far from here on the peak of Mount Sumeru there is a white lotus flower and a jade jug. If you have the courage to find your way to that mountain and reach its peak you will overcome all the dangers and difficulties that plague this world. If you bring this flower and jug back here and study and meditate, you will one day become a Bodhisattva and your wish to help others will be realized.'

Maio Shan did not have a chance to speak for the Buddha immediately turned back into a statue. His words, however, had given her new hope and she summoned her maid, Yung Lien, to help her make hasty preparations for the unknown dangers that might face them. After leaving a message for Maio Shan's father the two women set off. They wore thick straw shoes on their feet and on their shoulders they carried baskets containing food and cooking utensils.

A month after leaving the palace they were passing through the foothills of a mountain range when the sky above them was darkened by a flock of crows that swooped lower and lower towards them. Yung Lien screamed hysterically, afraid that these black, swiftly darting birds were going to gouge out her eyes, but Maio Shan calmed her.

'There's no need to worry. These birds wouldn't do this unless they had a reason. Unpack some food and throw it on the ground because I'm sure they're hungry.'

Yung Lien slung her basket and rummaged in it until she found a large bowl of cold rice which she threw on the ground in front of her. As Maio Shan had foreseen, the crows had only seemed threatening because they were hungry and after pecking up every grain of rice they rose in unison and flew away to the east. Yung Lien marvelled at her mistress's compassion at a time when they were both footsore and hungry.

At the end of the second month of their travels they came across a dense forest and fearlessly Maio Shan led them into the dark undergrowth. Whenever the sunlight managed to pierce the branches and reach the forest floor they caught sight of wonders they had only heard about from travelling storytellers. Animals of many shapes, sizes and patterns darted in and out of the shadows as if being chased by some invisible force and occasionally they caught a glimpse of small, powerful men dressed in strange animal skins.

As they approached a cleared patch of undergrowth a forest dweller entered the opposite side of the clearing, roaring with anguish as he carried a wounded friend. Once again Yung Lien was afraid that she might be attacked but Maio Shan ordered her to stand still and remain silent.

'What makes you think we're going to be hurt?' she inquired. 'This man is wounded and he needs our help.'

Maio Shan pulled her unwilling maid into the clearing

and together they bathed the man's deep and bloody cuts. Although the two forest dwellers did not speak in the presence of the women, Maio Shan saw that their feet had been ripped and deformed from a lifetime of hunting in the undergrowth and she offered them their straw sandals. The men accepted them, examined them carefully and bowed in thanks. Without a word being spoken the stronger man lifted his wounded friend into his arms and the two left the clearing.

Maio Shan and Yung Lien continued their travels in search of Mount Sumeru. Their provisions had run out after seventy days and they survived on wild fruit and berries, and since they no longer had shoes they wrapped leaves around their feet. Although the food did not satisfy their hunger or the leaves protect their feet, the two women continued their search with a will of iron and six months after they had set out they arrived at Mount Sumeru.

The most difficult part of the journey lay ahead, for the boulder-strewn slopes were steep and the snowy peak seemed to reach to the heavens. It took three arduous days of climbing to reach the summit and as they stood in the snow the Buddha once more appeared. In his left hand he held a translucent jade water jug and in his right hand rested a bright white lotus flower.

'My good children, you have proved your dedication on this long journey and I know you're ready to take my gift,' the Buddha said in a voice that seemed to fill Heaven and earth. 'You must take this jug and flower back to the palace and place them in front of the altar in your shrine. Each day you must make offerings to Heaven and develop wisdom through meditation and understanding. If you do this you will discover one day that the jade jug is full of water and a willow branch will grow out of this water. That will be the day that you will rise to Heaven and become a Bodhisattva.'

The Buddha dissolved into thin air without leaving any trace in the snow to show where he had been.

Maio Shan and Yung Lien descended the mountain and started their three month journey home. When they arrived at the palace they rejected the luxuries of the royal apartments and slept on simple straw beds in the temple precincts. Maio Shan placed the jade jug in front of a statue of the Buddha and the lotus flower in a pool in the temple courtyard. Each day she sat before the altar chanting a sutra to bring harmony to all living creatures.

Two years passed and many people from the kingdom came to talk to her and to meditate beside her and during all that time the lotus flower was in full bloom. Yung Lien told every visitor the promise that the Buddha had made and they anxiously awaited the moment that Maio Shan would ascend to Heaven, but the jade jug remained empty.

A local boy, Shan Ying, who enjoyed playing pranks, regularly slipped into the temple precincts to play in the gardens. Many people complained to Maio Shan that he was a useless urchin but she let him stay because he seemed happy to pass his time there. He mocked Yung Lien when she told him the story of the jade jug and the willow branch and one day he hit upon a scheme to make Maio Shan look a fool. That night, when the temple was quiet, he stole into the shrine room, filled the jade jug with well water and placed a willow twig in the jug.

The following day was the 19th day of the 6th month and as usual Maio Shan rose at dawn to meditate before the Buddha. As she was preparing to leave her room a child's excited cry echoed through the temple.

'It's happened. I've seen it for myself,' shouted Shan Ying as he dashed in and out of the temple rooms. 'Today is the day our princess will become a Bodhisattva.'

His high pitched yells disturbed the servants and the royal family and soon they had crowded into Maio Shan's small room. As Shan Ying edged his way through the hushed, expectant crowd he heard Maio Shan speak to those around her.

'I had a strange dream last night. I dreamed that a boy had come to help me become a Bodhisattva. I couldn't see his face or hear his voice but I know that his actions changed my life.'

Maio Shan picked up the jade vase and sat beside the lily pool while those around her chanted sutras. A faint sound of music came from the farthest corner of the heavens and grew louder as it closed in on them. Shan Ying began to shake with fear as the lotus flower grew larger and larger till it almost filled the pool. The adults drew back as Maio Shan's body rose from the floor and floated down to settle gently amidst the petals of the lotus flower. She remained motionless for several minutes as the crowd fell to their knees and then the lotus flower uprooted itself from the pool and Maio Shan rose to Heaven.

'Thank you,' she cried to Shan Ying as she disappeared into the cloud.

Maio Shan was taken to Heaven and appointed Kuan Yin, Goddess of Mercy, by the Jade Emperor. Her maid remained on earth and at her death was given the title Dragon Girl, maid to the Goddess of Mercy.

Kuan Yin has the power to travel wherever she wishes and take whatever form is appropriate to help those in need. Sometimes she is an old woman, sometimes a young woman and at other times a young girl. When the land is dry she stands on a cloud and dips the willow stick into the water in the jade jug and sprinkles it on the earth. Wherever there is pain or suffering Kuan Yin can be found, and her image adorns the homes and temples of rich and poor alike.

Yo Lung Mountain

Many years ago Pai Li village in western China was struck by a drought so severe that the earth cracked and the rivers dried up. The village was named after the white pear trees that grew in abundance in that area, but after six months without rain their roots had shrivelled up.

Yo Lung lived in this village with his blind mother and his sole source of income, as well as that of the other villagers, was the white pear crop. He knew that it was useless to sit at home in the hope that the sky would rain rice and so, armed with a knife, he set off to the mountains to find edible grass roots. He walked many miles over hot earth and sharp stones but even the mountain grass had been unable to survive the drought. Exhausted from his search he sat on the edge of a cliff to rest. The sound of a woman weeping and sighing was carried by the wind to where he sat.

'Who is it? Who's down there?' he shouted, surprised that anyone should be found in this lonely spot.

There was no reply to his question but he could still hear the woman crying and he began the hazardous descent. The moon was rising in the east by the time he reached the dark cave at the base of the cliff from where the cries came. He lit a torch of dry brushwood, took a deep breath and entered the cave. He immediately spotted a white-haired old woman crouched on the floor and as he drew closer he saw the reason for her tears. An iron chain had been wrapped around both her feet and secured to a massive rock in the far corner of the cave.

'Old woman, why are you here? Are you a ghost?' asked Yo Lung, more surprised than frightened.

The old woman was trembling as she replied. 'I'm not a ghost or an evil spirit. I'm the wife of the Sea Dragon King and my home is on the ocean floor. It was my job to travel to Heaven every day to make the rain fall but one day I was busy talking to the Jade Emperor and I allowed too much rain to fall. As a result the earth was flooded and my husband was so furious that he hit me three hundred times with a dragon cudgel and then banished me here for four hundred years.'

She stopped speaking and began to cry quietly, her whole body shaking with each sob.

'Please stop crying,' implored Yo Lung. 'I'll find a way to save you. I promise I won't leave until you're free.'

'If you have time, there is a way,' replied the old woman. 'If you climb to the top of the cliff you will find a hu tree which is three thousand years old. You must pluck three thousand dry leaves from the tree but make sure that the leaves are exactly the same size as the palm of your hand. Bring the leaves here and burn them under the iron chain. The heat and the smoke from the leaves will dissolve the chain.'

Yo Lung did not need any encouragement to do as the old woman had asked and, without a thought for the dangers lurking on the dark cliff, he started his ascent. The gnarled hu tree was easy to find but it took him all night and all morning to find the right-sized leaves. He bundled them into his jacket and once more set off down the cliff. By the time he arrived back in the cave his clothes were ripped and the skin of his hands and feet was torn and bleeding. Nevertheless he lit the fire and waited beside the old woman throughout the following night. The chain dissolved at daybreak the next day.

The old woman slowly rose to her feet and as she squeezed Yo Lung's hands in gratitude she promised him enough riches to reach the ceiling of the cave. Yo Lung listened impassively as she described the priceless gems she would give him but her voice trailed off as soon as she noticed the blank look on his face.

'I'm sorry, I don't want to reject your kindness,' said Yo Lung quickly, 'but money doesn't interest me. It's more important that you grant me three wishes. Would that be possible?'

The old woman nodded in agreement and Yo Lung continued, 'My mother has been blind for ten years. Can you heal her?'

The old woman nodded in affirmation and Yo Lung put forward his two remaining requests. 'I would like you to make the fruit trees in our garden fruitful again and then will you bring the rain to our village so that the pear trees will flower once more?'

When the old woman heard this request she shook her head in doubt. She could have fulfilled any request in the world except this one since she had been forbidden to produce rain for more than four hundred years. But she also knew that it was her duty to repay Yo Lung and so she took a small crystal ball and a bowl from a deep fold in her skirt. She held the ball over the bowl and, after offering prayers to Heaven, shook the ball three times. With each shake a jet of water streamed like sunlight from the bottom of the ball into the bowl. She replaced the ball in her belt and handed the bowl to Yo Lung.

'Use this immortality water to wash your mother's eyes

and then take a mouthful and swallow it. When you have
done that, take a second mouthful and spit it across your
back garden. But I must warn you, if you take more
than two mouthfuls of water you will turn into a frog. A
fourth mouthful will cause your death by drowning. You
must realize that I can change your fortune but I cannot
change the future of your village. Take note of my warning. If you disobey me you will never see your mother
again.'

As Yo Lung returned home the old woman's warning
and the villagers' pleas whirled round and round in his
head. When he told his mother what had happened she
advised him to do what ever he thought was right. On
hearing this advice Yo Lung fell on his knees and kow-
towed three times in front of her. He did not need to say
anything for they both knew that this was the last time
they would be together. He then washed his mother's eyes
with the water and her sight was restored. Next he took
two mouthfuls of water and spat them into his back garden.
As he had expected, the trees immediately began to sprout
leaves and buds. Then aware of the fate that lay ahead of
him, he ran to the mountain facing Pai Li village with the
crystal dish of water. He took two more mouthfuls of water
and spat them high into the sky. The water hung in the
air until a huge black cloud formed itself like an umbrella
and then the rain fell with a fury that left the fields water-
logged for weeks.

While the villagers congratulated one another, the
ground underneath Yo Lung's feet opened up and swallowed him with the speed of lightning. There was nothing
that anyone could do to save him, but at the very moment
that the earth closed again a stream of water spouted from
the spot where he had disappeared. Even in times of
drought that spring continues to flow and irrigate the crops
of Pai Li, and it is said that the water is the gift of Yo
Lung. Throughout China the mountain is known as Yo

Lung and the stream which never dries up is known as the Immortality Stream.

Dragon Gate Mountain

Ta Yu was employed by the government as an inspector of watercourses, rivers, ditches and dykes. If rivers failed to flow, if the force of water was too great, or if the flow of the river needed diverting, Ta Yu was the first man the government would contact. After thirteen years of skilled practice he had won respect from the people and favour from the gods.

One day Ta Yu was summoned to Dragon Gate Mountain in Shansi province. A fast-flowing river hit the north side of the mountain with great force, lashing against boulders and flooding the fields. Then it flowed around the base of the mountain and continued its course on the south side. Ta Yu was ordered to build a tunnel through the mountain linking the flow of the river in the north with its course in the south.

Ta Yu visited the mountain many times to work out the best way to drill a hole through the stone and block the course of the old river. He even slept there to see if he could find inspiration. Eventually he drew up a plan which he hoped would work and he was given a team of three hundred men to complete the task.

From the first day the project was plagued by accidents: the stone drills broke on contact with the mountain, the flow of the water increased and many men were thrown to their deaths in the swirling vortex on the north side. Ta Yu did not expect his men to undertake anything he would not do himself and so he put his life at risk every moment of the day. The government, however, was determined to construct the tunnel and after the loss of many lives a large deep chamber had been hollowed out of the hillside.

One evening, when all the workers had returned home, Ta Yu walked along the base of the mountain to examine the work. As he inspected each stage of the tunnel he sighed with satisfaction, happy to see the project completed and happy to know that hundreds of lives would be saved in the future. He walked away from the tunnel along a path that wound up the mountain but he was so deep in thought he did not notice where he was going. At one moment the evening sun warmed his body and at the next the chill damp air made him shiver.

He had inadvertently entered a cave which he had never seen before. Ahead of him lay a tunnel, lit by eerie shafts of light, that seemed to extend for miles and miles into the mountain. Something had compelled him to enter the cave and as soon as he started walking through the narrow, low-roofed tunnel all thoughts of the outside world disappeared from his mind. At first he was able to pick his way across the rough stone floor, guided by the shafts of light, but one by one they disappeared and he was left to stumble through the darkness. Eventually it became so dark he could no longer see anything and so he turned around and groped his way back along the tunnel. He had lost all sense of time but when he finally emerged from the cave, the first stars of evening had appeared.

The next morning Ta Yu left his men, returned to the

cave with an oil lamp and retraced his footsteps. The walls
were uneven and damp and he occasionally caught sight
of small characters scratched on the grey stone, but he
could not understand what they represented. After walking
for more than an hour, the light from his lamp fell across
a sleeping animal crouched against the tunnel wall. It
looked like a pig but it had a strange yellow tint to its skin
and in its mouth it held a bright, perfectly rounded pearl.

Ta Yu edged his way farther along the tunnel and then
caught sight of a ferocious-looking green dog, crouched
low as though ready to pounce. Ta Yu froze immediately,
but the dog did nothing more than bark for a minute as
if trying to speak to him. Then it rose and began to walk
deeper into the mountain. Meanwhile the pig had been
awakened from its sleep and stood behind Ta Yu, who
was left with no choice but to follow the dog.

All three walked in silence for miles and miles. Ta Yu
had lost all sense of time and direction and although he
expected to feel tired his body seemed weightless. The
farther he walked the healthier he felt, until he saw a
bright white light ahead of him and his limbs suddenly
felt laden with iron.

The dog stopped abruptly, swung around and turned
its piercing green eyes on Ta Yu. While the dog held Ta
Yu's attention the pig began to change shape. Its yellow
skin became darker and its fore and hind legs became the
legs and arms of a man. Finally the dog moved its head
to stare at the apparition and Ta Yu followed its gaze.
The pig had turned into a man wearing black robes. At
that very moment the dog also changed its form and it too
became a man dressed in flowing black robes. Although
a word had not been spoken Ta Yu knew that he stood
before two of the Jade Emperor's servants.

Ta Yu looked beyond the servants towards the patch of
bright white light ahead of him. He saw a man with the
face of a snake and the body of a human sitting in the
circle of light. Without fear or trepidation Ta Yu moved

towards this figure and realized that he was in the presence of one of the gods. The deity lifted a parchment scroll from the floor beside him, beckoned Ta Yu to come even closer and unravelled the scroll on the stone floor. Eight groups of lines had been drawn in black ink: some were broken and others were complete, and Ta Yu recognized the lines immediately as the Eight Hexagrams.

'Are you the sage who was born to the goddess Wah Su?' Ta Yu asked.

'Yes, I am,' replied the deity. 'My mother lived in a perfect land and one day, when travelling alone through this land, she was surrounded for two hours by a rainbow. The Jade Emperor sent a baby down the rainbow to my mother and after twelve years I was born.'

While the god spoke Ta Yu had time to recall the legends his mother had taught him as a child and it slowly dawned on him that he stood face to face with an Emperor who had once ruled China. At realization he fell to his knees in salute.

The Emperor turned round and lifted up a jade tablet, twelve inches in length. Each inch represented one of the twelve divisions of the day and one of the twelve units of the calendar. The Emperor handed the tablet to Ta Yu with these words. 'The tunnel through the Dragon Gate Mountain was your final test and so far you have performed it well. The gods of Heaven have decided that the time is right for you to govern China. The hexagrams on this chart will help you to predict the fortunate years for your people and the jade tablet will give you the authority to judge wisely. Not even the most learned sage will doubt your wisdom.'

Ta Yu accepted the gifts of the gods with humility and left the immortal still bathed in a circle of light. Guided by the Jade Emperor's servants, he returned to the outside world and to his work of building a tunnel through Dragon Gate Mountain.

The tunnel was soon finished to popular acclaim from

poor and rich alike and, as the immortal Emperor had foretold, Ta Yu was himself declared Emperor. According to legend he ruled wisely for forty years and during his reign the land was never plagued by drought, famine or flood.

The Silver Pot and the Boiling Sea

To Lo, who lived in the palace of Heaven across the Eastern Sea, was the god in charge of refining and mixing magical elixirs. One day the silence of his workroom was broken by the high, piercing cry of a crane which flew in through the open window. The crane circled three times over To Lo's head, dropped a letter from its beak onto the floor and then flew out of the window. To Lo halted his experiments to open this unexpected missive.

The letter was from Hsi Wang Mu, a heavenly princess who lived on K'unlun Mountain and who was reputed to have hundreds of spirits under her command. The letter read:

My dear To Lo,

I recently held a party on Yau Ch'ih Lake to celebrate my birthday. During the evening Chin Tung and Yu Nu, my servant boy and my maid, drank too much immortal wine. After breaking several pitchers of wine and insulting my guests, they disappeared for three days. They have now returned and apologized but, nevertheless, it is my duty to punish them. I propose to turn

114

Chin Tung into a human and send Yu Nu down to the palace of the Sea Dragon King. It will be many years before I let them meet again and marry. When the time comes will you release their souls and return them to me?

I trust you will obey my orders.

Your friend,
Hsi Wang Mu

To Lo put the letter safely away and continued with his experiments, certain that the goddess would contact him when she needed his help.

As the goddess had warned, Chin Tung was transformed into a baby boy and placed by the goddess in the Chang family. His parents, unaware of his true identity, named him Chang Yu and brought him up to be an honourable and well-educated boy. At the age of twenty-two his parents died and Chang Yu took his inheritance, left the family home and travelled throughout China visiting the temples and monasteries his tutor had so often talked about.

Chang Yu was particularly drawn to an isolated temple built on the shores of the Eastern Sea and he decided to stay and study with the master of the temple. On the first evening, after study and meditation, he took his lute from his small travelling bag and sat on the shore facing the Eastern Sea. The sea was calm and the moon full as he played a haunting melody that his father had taught him as a boy. The soft notes floated through the night, across the lake and melted into the dark water.

The melody reached the ears of a young girl, Yu Lien, in the Sea Dragon's palace. According to the palace servants, she had been discovered on the sea floor by one of the crab guards and taken to the palace where she had been adopted by the Sea Dragon King. Yu Lien was unaware of her true identity and had long forgotten the day that she and Chin Tung had been expelled from Heaven.

Yu Lien was entranced by the faint strands of music that came from far above her and she left the palace to search for its source. Carefully avoiding the crabs who guarded the palace gates, she rose to the surface and swam to the shore. Stealthily she approached the sandy bank where Chang Yu was playing and lay down in a hollow close to him so she could listen to the music.

Suddenly a string on the lute snapped and Chang Yu jumped back to avoid its catching his fingers. He heard a rustle in the sand at his side and looked up quickly to catch sight of a beautiful girl staring at him. For a moment their eyes were transfixed on each other and then Yu Lien jumped to her feet, ran to the sea and disappeared beneath the surface. In pursuit Chang Yu stumbled across the sea shore but tripped over a sharp object on the sand. Yu Lien was deep beneath the surface by the time he reached the water but the sharp object that had caused his fall gave him hope; it was a jade brooch from her dress.

That night Chang Yu slept with the jade brooch beside him and the following day he wandered up and down the shore hoping to catch sight of the girl. He waited until sunset and then turned back to the temple. At that moment a Taoist priest appeared by his side and asked him why he looked so sad. Chang Yu was glad of someone to talk to. After recounting his story he produced the jade brooch as evidence.

'I don't think you realize how important this piece of jade is,' said the priest as he examined it in detail. 'It belongs to a Sea Dragon princess and she would not have left it behind unless she wanted to see you again.'

'Please help me find her again. I'll do anything to see her once more,' pleaded Chang Yu.

The Taoist priest took hold of Chang Yu's arm to calm him down.

'Now don't become too excited,' he advised. 'If you are determined to see her again, you have to understand her father, the Sea Dragon King. He has a furious temper and if you anger him you will never live to tell this story to anyone else. Even the sight of him is enough to make many gods and immortals shake. He has a long, dark-green face and two huge teeth that protrude over his lower lip. He is capable of sucking into his body anything that annoys him, even people or buildings that are at the most distant corners of the earth. He can bite through stone and tear gold with his teeth, and the weight of his body is enough to kill a hundred men. He is strong enough to send a wave higher than the highest mountain crashing onto the shore, a wave that would swallow every ship at sea and engulf every village in its path. Do you still want to pursue the Sea Dragon's daughter?'

'If I thought there was a way to reach her I would still pursue her. After what you say I know I would be killed as soon as I entered the sea, but I'm still not ready to abandon hope.'

The Taoist priest was impressed with the young man's determination to find Yu Lien and realized that fate had predetermined that this couple should see each other again. He knelt down in the sand and unstrapped a leather bag at his feet. There were many strange objects in the bag but the priest chose three in particular: a silver pot, a brass ladle and a gold coin. He handed them to Chang Yu with these instructions, 'Fill this ladle with sea water, pour the water into the silver pot and then place the coin in the pot. Heat the pot over a stove and as soon as the water begins to boil the sea will also boil. For every tenth of an inch that the water evaporates, the sea level will drop by ten feet. When the pot has boiled dry the seabed will be exposed. That is the time to strike, for the Sea Dragon King will be at his most vulnerable.'

After giving his instructions the Taoist priest left Chang Yu alone to carry out the plan. The young man collected loose brushwood from the shore and built a fire, over which he placed the silver pot. When the pot began to simmer he eagerly piled more and more brushwood on the fire to make the water boil as quickly as possible. As the water began to boil the surface of the sea also began to bubble and before long it was covered with thick steam. The heat was so great that even Chang Yu began to sweat and soon the silence was shattered by the screaming of hordes of crabs and prawns, boiled bright red by the heat, dashing for the cool sand.

Just then an old Buddhist monk ran up to Chang Yu and begged him to stop, 'You're the cause of this disaster. Stop it at once. A few minutes ago the Sea Dragon's guards rushed to see me and asked me to find the man responsible for this havoc. The Sea Dragon King is willing to give you whatever you want but you must stop boiling the sea water.'

'Don't make a fool of me, how could I possibly swim down to the bottom of the sea? It's far too deep,' replied Chang Yu angrily.

'Don't worry,' said the Buddhist monk calmly. 'Just follow me and I promise that not a drop of water will touch you.'

Chang Yu obeyed the monk and extinguished the fire. As soon as the water cooled down, the steam over the sea disappeared and the water level rose once again. The Buddhist monk led Chang Yu down to the sea shore and pointed his wooden staff towards the sea. The waters began to heave and huge waves lashed against each other; slowly the watery mass separated to form two huge walls of water, leaving a path over the seabed. The two men walked over the dry seabed until they arrived at the stone-encrusted palace which was usually hidden from human view.

The four vicious-eyed lobsters who guarded the palace doors stood aside as they approached and the heavy coral gates were slowly swung open by two plodding turtles. The palace walls were opulently decorated with precious stones and the silk curtains were laden with translucent pearls. Coral lamps illuminated by crystal balls hung from the ceiling and the furniture was carved out of gold, jade and ivory.

After passing through twenty chambers they finally reached the throne room where the Sea Dragon King sat mopping his brow with a large yellow sponge. He beckoned to them to sit down on stools in front of him but he was too hot and agitated to offer greetings. The king lifted a spiral shell to his mouth and blew one long, deep, piercing note which resounded through the palace, and before Chang Yu could turn round to see what was happening six mermaids escorted his beloved Yu Lien to the king's throne.

'You don't have to tell me that you have fallen in love with my daughter. My fish spies have told me already,' said the king still panting from the heat. 'I don't want to waste any time so, as ruler of the Eastern Sea, I give my permission for my daughter to become your wife. You must worship Heaven and earth and your bond will be sealed for eternity. Now someone bring me wine to help me cool down.'

A spiral shell brimming with wine was placed in the king's hand and the wedding celebrations began in earnest. Several hours later everyone in the palace had managed to squeeze into the throne-room to dance, drink and sing, but the noise and bustle were quickly silenced by the tolling of a bell beside the king's throne.

To Lo had descended from Heaven to fulfil Hsi Wang Mu's orders. He stood on a carpet of cloud and spoke to the attentive crowd, who pushed forward to hear the story of the newlyweds' real identity, their misdemeanour in Heaven and their subsequent punishment. If anything, this made Chang Yu and Yu Lien even more popular with the wedding crowd and once more they were toasted with shells of wine. But while the crowd prepared for the toast, To Lo poured a magic elixir into the wine shells. As Chang Yu and Yu Lien swallowed the wine they felt their bodies lose all sense of weight and the cheerful sounds and vivid colours of the palace floated before their eyes. To fond farewells from the crab guards, prawns, turtles and starfish, Chang Yu and Yu Lien were carried home by To Lo.

The young couple were greeted on their return to Heaven by Hsi Wang Mu, who had forgiven them many years ago. They had proved their worth during their exile on earth and were granted positions of authority in her household. Each time fairies or spirits returned to K'unlun Mountain after working on earth Chang Yu and Yu Lien were there to greet them. It is said that even today they are sometimes glimpsed feeding wandering spirits on K'unlun Mountain.

The Child No One Wanted

Thousands of years ago the people of China did not know how to plough the land or grow crops; they relied completely on hunting for their survival. Every summer they formed hunting parties and organized week-long trips into the forests and mountains. Successful hunts enabled the people to survive throughout the winter and the rainy season, but if the hunters failed to kill enough animals hundreds of people died in the winter months. They believed that their fate depended upon the god of Heaven and so they worshipped him every morning and evening.

At that time the Princess Consort of the Emperor was a girl of ten called Chiang Yuan. She was clever, hardworking and dutiful. Every morning and evening she prayed to the god of Heaven asking him to bestow good fortune on the people.

One morning, when she was praying to the god of Heaven on a wild, barren hillside, she noticed a set of footprints leading as far as she could see. Startled by their enormous length and width, she bent over them to compare their size with that of her tiny feet. The whole of her foot could fit into the toe of one footprint. Intrigued but not afraid, she followed the footprints over the mountain and down the far side into a valley. They stopped abruptly at a solitary rock on a windy outcrop dotted with wild grass. She searched the area for evidence of a secret hiding place but there was nothing strange or unusual about the place, and satisfied that she was safe, she fell asleep against the rock.

Her sleep was disturbed by a vivid dream in which a clear voice spoke to her, 'I am the god of Heaven and I have listened to you every morning and every evening. You are young but you have enough strength to carry out the mission that I will now give you.'

Chiang Yuan knelt down in her dream and respectfully asked what the god of Heaven intended for her.

'You will know soon,' replied the god, and that was all he said.

Chiang Yuan tried to catch a glimpse of the god but all she could see was a shadow. She had to shield her eyes from the dazzling light. She called out to him, but he had gone, and she awoke with her hands still protecting her eyes.

By now it was almost dark and a biting wind swept across the rocky outcrop where she lay. She made her way back guided by the light of the stars and the deep depressions left by the footprints. She felt as though the dream had given her renewed energy and in the following days, instead of fading from her memory, the events of the dream became more vivid.

Exactly nine months after the god of Heaven spoke to her she gave birth to a son, but as she was not yet married everyone in the palace, from the servants to the Emperor, interpreted this as a bad omen. The child was considered evil and no one except the princess was willing to touch him because they believed he would bring disaster. Chiang Yuan was too young to fight for her child and was unable to stop the Emperor ordering him to be abandoned. Her family took the child to a cold, uninhabited spot, but before leaving him to die they named him Ch'i, the name given to anything useless that should be thrown away.

The family did not notice that a herd of cattle was grazing close to the spot where they left the child. As Ch'i lay on the ground that first cold night, the oxen lay down beside him to protect him and the cows offered him their milk. Four days later a team of hunters from the palace was walking across this wild spot when they heard the cries of a baby and discovered to their dismay that the child who heralded misfortune for the kingdom was still alive. Intent on letting him die, they placed him in a leather sling and took him deep into a forest so dense that the rays of the sun were unable to penetrate its branches. They laid Ch'i on a bed of damp leaves where he would be easy prey for the poisonous snakes that slithered through the rotting vegetation.

The god of Heaven took care of Ch'i, and a woodcutter, working on the edge of the forest, heard the child's cries echoing eerily through the trees. He ran home to fetch an oil lamp and returned to the forest where he eventually found the baby lying near a hollow tree. Before he could pick him up a python slithered down the trunk and gazed greedily at the baby, every now and then darting its flickering tongue towards the crying bundle. For more than fifteen minutes the python threatened to attack but an invisible force protected the child and the snake kept its distance. This tense scene was disturbed by the approach of a tiger, and the snake recoiled to a position of safety on a branch.

In turn the hungry tiger prowled around the baby licking its lips in anticipation, but it too did not dare to touch the child and eventually it slipped away in search of food elsewhere.

All this time the woodcutter remained hidden in the undergrowth and witnessed the whole scene in amazed silence. Now that the animals had retreated and the forest was silent he ran to the child, placed him gently in his woven blanket and took him home.

Even in the woodcutter's house the child was in danger when word of this strange baby reached the Emperor. The stories confirmed the Emperor's suspicions about the child and a troop of guards was dispatched to take the child from the woodcutter. The guards were afraid to kill the baby in case they should be struck down by an evil spell and so they abandoned him on the icy bank of a river where he was sure to freeze before nightfall.

The riverside birds and animals were sheltering from the bitter cold and there was no living creature moving on the icy banks to help him. Once again the god of Heaven intervened and a group of seagulls flew over the spot where the baby lay. Their sharp eyes caught sight of Ch'i, even though his white gown blended with the ice around him, and they swooped down to protect him with their wings. They kept him warm throughout the night and were prepared to stay with him a second night but they were frightened off by an arrow fired in their direction by a local hunter. Aware that they would be easy prey if they stayed with the child, they flew away to a safer destination.

When the seagulls had gone the wind rose and Ch'i cried loudly as the bitter cold bit into his bones. The hunter was drawn to his cries and, aware that the child had been left for dead, he took him home and gave him a place in his family. The hunter had not heard the stories of the child of ill omen born to the Princess Consort and Ch'i was raised as the hunter's own son.

Many years later Ch'i worked alone every day on the windswept hills and in deserted valleys around his village. Through experience he learned which plants were poisonous and which were safe; he taught himself how to cultivate seeds and crops; and he knew when to plant and when to leave the land fallow. Over the years he had turned a rank wilderness into fruitful, well-tended land. Everyone in the area, even the oldest and wisest, was drawn to his valley to learn the secrets of agriculture from Ch'i. His knowledge was spread from province to province and soon every valley and plain was brimming with rice, beans, peas, hemp, wheat and melon.

Men were willing to walk for weeks on end to be taught by Ch'i and he soon came to be recognized as the divine intermediary between Heaven and earth. Every day the villagers offered sacrifices of thanks to the god of Heaven, and when they boiled rice they allowed the steam to rise to the sky as a sign of gratitude. Ch'i eventually left his home village and travelled the country, farming, teaching, studying and raising his own family. Many years later, the Chou dynasty, his descendants, came to the throne of China. Under his guidance the land prospered and bore a generous harvest for each year of their reign.

The First Cat

Long ago, when the world was newly created, there were thousands of animals but only two human beings and a single devil living on the earth. The humans worked hard by day to grow enough food to survive but when night fell they retreated to their house leaving the wild animals to hunt in peace. On the other hand, the devil hated the daylight and cowered in his dark, damp cave until nightfall, when he set out to create as much evil as possible until dawn.

The humans hated the scheming devil; the trees and plants were scared of him; even the gods disliked him and were loathe to confront him. But the devil did not care what the rest of creation thought of him for he had his army of corrupt mice and he knew that nothing, not even the powers of Heaven, could destroy him.

One fine day, when the plants were in full flower and the world seemed to be at peace, the devil lurked in the shadowy entrance of his cave trying to think of something to do. As his gaze fell upon the point where the horizon linked the sky and the earth he hit upon an ingenious plan. He knew that the horizon had been created by the god of Heaven to keep the sky and the earth securely together. He had heard the humans say that if the horizon disappeared the sky would float away and the earth would turn upside down and roll away into endless time. And he thought to himself, how interesting it would be to see what would really happen if the horizon was destroyed.

When night fell the devil summoned his mice soldiers for a tactical meeting. When they had finally gathered in their ranks before him they rested on their hind legs and listened attentively to their master's plan.

'I've asked you to do many things in the past but today I've hit upon my most destructive plan ever.' He pointed at the horizon, dimly visible by the light of the full moon. Then he gave a cunning smile and added, 'I want you to gnaw through the horizon before dawn. I want it completely destroyed by the first light of day. Is that clear? Now move!'

The mice squealed with delight and rushed off towards the distant horizon. They arrived three hours before dawn and set to work with a vengeance. Although their mouths were small, their teeth were sharp, and by dawn the sky and earth were only attached to the horizon by weak, half-chewed threads. The mice ran for cover before the sun hit their backs and took shelter in the damp cave.

The man and the woman awoke earlier than usual, disturbed by the slight but perceptible shaking of the earth. They ran from their beds to be greeted by the terrifying sight of the earth and the sky moving apart from each other. For a moment they were silent, afraid that they might die at any moment, and then they realized that it was up to them to save the world. The man ran into the house to gather thick iron needles and strong thread, hard-wearing enough to withstand hurricanes and typhoons. It took all day to repair the horizon, and even then it was still lumpy and patchy, but they had done their best and the earth and sky were once more secure.

They returned home exhausted but as they approached the house they heard a loud sound of shuffling and squealing coming from their storeroom. In retaliation for their efforts to repair the sky, the devil had sent a troop of rats to the storeroom to demolish their entire food supply. Infuriated by the writhing black creatures, the man grabbed a stout walking stick and the woman an iron shovel and they fearlessly beat the rats. Some made a hasty escape but the mangled bodies of others lay scattered on the floor. Too tired to clear away the bodies, the couple went to bed and slept soundly.

When they awoke the next morning they ran to the window to check the sky was still in place, and it was. But their hearts sank when they gazed at their fields of rice, for during the night the rats had eaten the whole crop. Aware that they would die unless they protected their few remaining vegetables, they decided to beg the god of the Horizon to help them.

The man and the woman lit joss sticks and offered baskets of fruit to the god of the Horizon, whose statue had pride of place in their house shrine. They knelt before him and begged his help. A mist slowly descended on the altar and a resonant voice rang out from the statue.

'I have been waiting for you to come to me. Thank you for saving my horizon – it will never be destroyed again. You have no need to worry about the mice because I know a way to keep them under control. Look for a cat. When you have found one let it share your home and lands with you, and you will never be troubled by mice again.'

'But what is a cat and where can we find one?' asked the woman in despair.

The god of the Horizon hesitated for a moment, then replied, 'Well, I know that there is a cat in Heaven, but I don't know where you can find one on earth. I know that the tiger is familiar with all the animals on earth. Perhaps he could help you. I wish you good fortune.'

The god's voice faded from the room and the mist lifted from the shrine.

The man and the woman knew that a tiger lived in a cave not far from their home but they had always kept a safe distance from him and he had never bothered them. This was the first time they had dared speak to such a respected and powerful animal and so they approached his cave with trepidation. The tiger sat outside sunning himself and barely lifted his head as they drew near, but he raised his paw and beckoned them to sit in front of him. The couple timidly sat on the floor so close that they could see their reflection in the tiger's large yellow eyes.

'How can I help you?' growled the tiger.

'We're sorry to disturb you,' replied the man, 'but the devil's mice are on the verge of starving us to death and we need to find a cat. That's why we've come to you.'

'A cat, you're looking for a cat, are you?' repeated the tiger, purring to himself. 'I don't have a cat here but I can make one for you. If you wait a moment I'll produce one.'

The tiger scratched the side of his body with his sharp black claws and continued to scratch until he had made a hole deep enough to reveal his liver. The tiger then curled up and, without wincing, pulled his liver out of his body. He calmly placed the liver in front of the man and the woman and sealed the gash in his body with wax.

'Take this liver and go home with it. This is your cat.'

'Thank you very much,' replied the husband in surprise. 'I've never seen a cat before and I believe what you say, but how can a liver-shaped cat chase a mouse? Surely the mice will eat the liver instead of the liver eating them.'

'Believe what I say. This is a cat. Take it home and you will never be troubled with mice problems again. Now please leave me to rest,' roared the annoyed tiger.

The man and the woman did not dare to disobey him so they wrapped the liver in straw matting and left the cave as quickly as possible. On the way home, while they were discussing what they should do, the woman felt something wriggle in the straw matting. She placed the mat on the floor and unrolled it to reveal a brown- and gold-mottled cat, who rubbed itself against their legs and purred contentedly.

'This must be a cat!' cried the man excitedly. 'Hurry up, let's take it home so we can see what the mice think of it.'

The minute they entered the rice fields the cat jumped from the woman's arms and darted to and fro across the field, mewing with delight. Every now and then it tossed a mouse in the air and caught it again in its claws. The mice fled in terror and word soon spread among the devil's army of the predator waiting for them at the man and woman's house.

This is why mice keep a safe distance from any house where a cat lives and explains why a cat looks so like a tiger.

Five Men Mountains

Shu state in Szechuan was ruled by a king who was greedy and lazy. He left the affairs of state to ministers and spent half his time thinking of new ways to increase his wealth and the other half experimenting with magical elixirs in search of eternal life. The states that bordered his kingdom were continually warring with one another but they did not dare attack Shu state since it was protected by five giants who could uproot trees with one hand, demolish a house with a single kick and knock a man off his feet just by whistling.

Ch'in state lay to the north of Shu state but the only access between the two was through a narrow gorge surrounded by steep mountains. This difficult pass and the threat of the giants had prevented the ambitious king of Ch'in state from launching an attack, but he, more than any of the neighbouring rulers, was determined to incorporate Shu state into his kingdom.

After months of thought the king of Ch'in state hit upon a plan to weaken his neighbour's defences. He ordered the palace stonemasons to construct five monumental stone cows out of a solid block of stone hewn from the mountainside. When the stonemasons' work was finished the cows were hauled with ramps and pulleys to the entrance of the narrow gorge and a block of gold was placed behind each cow. The king of Ch'in state then ordered his spies to spread a rumour throughout Shu state that these cows were excreting huge blocks of gold each day. When word reached the king of Shu he immediately ordered a detachment of soldiers to guard the cows and sent a diplomatic mission to negotiate for them with the ruler of Ch'in.

The cows had been placed across the boundary between the two states so that each state had equal claim to them, but the ruler of Ch'in said he was willing to abandon his claim on the grounds that his state was larger and wealthier than his neighbour's. The king of Shu could not believe his good fortune and he ordered the giants to carry the cows to his palace, where they could live in comfort and continue to produce blocks of gold.

The giants raised the cows onto their shoulders and staggered towards the narrow gorge, but the gap between the mountains was too narrow and the giants collided against the trees and boulders with each step. Afraid that they would damage the precious cows, the giants decided to widen the gap so the cows could pass through safely. The cows were laid aside and the giants ripped the mountainsides apart with their bare hands. They hurled the trees into the neighbouring kingdom, blew the stones into the distance and tossed enormous lumps of rock into Ch'in state. When the gap was wide enough, the giants carried the five cows through on their shoulders and laid them in the palace courtyard.

The king of Ch'in state had achieved one objective, but now he had to find a way to destroy the giants who stood in his path. He had been told of a deadly thousand-year-old python who lived in the forest between the two states, and so he spread another rumour about a thousand-year-old snake whose eyes were so potent that, if eaten, they would give eternal life. When the king of Shu heard the new rumour he became obsessed with this new possibility of immortality.

The five giants were sent to capture the snake and tear out its eyes, and although they suspected that this was a trap, they could not argue with their ruler. After searching the forest the giants saw the huge tail of a python lying outside a cave. The tail was four feet wide and so powerful that one giant could not lift it alone. Two giants then tried to pull the python out of the cave but they could scarcely move it. They were joined by two more, but still the python would barely move. Eventually the fifth giant joined them and they tugged the python until its whole body was gradually exposed to the sun. The python lay motionless on the ground and the giants gingerly approached its head with the intention of tearing its eyes out.

Just as they were about to sink their sharp nails into the python's head, the snake shuddered with such force that the ground shook and the mountain above them quaked. Before the giants could run the snake slid back into the cave and enormous boulders came hurtling towards them. The air was filled with thunder as the mountain collapsed burying the giants under its mass. As the giants were crushed to death their bodies became harder and they slowly turned into five stone mountains.

When the king of Ch'in state heard of the giants' deaths he immediately launched an attack on Shu state but the king of Shu surrendered without a fight. To commemorate his victory the ruler of Ch'in renamed the gorge Gold Cow Gap and, in memory of the giants who sacrificed their lives, he named the place where they died Five Men Mountains, and that is how they are known to this day.

The Story of the Cockscomb

Long ago, a hunter lived in a secluded valley in the west of China. He hunted by day but spent each evening caring for the trees and plants which flourished in his garden and which he had tended lovingly since he was a boy.

One evening, on his return from a day's hunting, he discovered that his favourite mulberry bush had begun to wither. Afraid that the ground was diseased, he replanted the tree in freshly dug soil, spread a layer of manure around its roots and sprayed it with spring water.

'Tomorrow you will be healthy again,' he reassured the tree before going to bed.

The following morning he rushed out to examine his tree but its branches were weaker than the previous day and its fruit was rotten. The hunter knew that his mulberry tree was dying.

He desperately looked around to find the cause of this sickness but there was nothing in the neighbouring soil or on the neighbouring plants to suggest that they were responsible. He gazed up to the sun beating down on his plants and his question was answered.

'It's you, you've killed my mulberry tree,' he shouted
angrily, waving his fist at the sun, which shone back
impassively. 'Why have you done this? Why do you want
to kill my plants? You're so hot you'll destroy anything
that your rays touch. And it's not just you that is trying to
kill everything. Your friend the moon is no good – her
light is too strong as well.'

The hunter stormed back into his house and paced up
and down the room desperately trying to think of a way
to destroy the sun and the moon. He considered many
possibilities and finally decided to use his hunting bow
and arrow. The sun was in the middle of the sky when
the hunter took aim. He skilfully shot the arrow directly
at the sun. It flew high above the earth and reached its
target, piercing the sun's eye. The sun rolled in pain and
hid in the nearest cloud. Even though the clouds tried to
push him back into the sky again, he refused to show his
face and retreated deeper and deeper into the clouds until
his light was obscured from the earth.

Pleased with his kill, the hunter aimed for the moon,
which had been woken from her sleep by the sudden
darkness. She edged her way into the sky and prepared
for the night's work, but as soon as she showed her face
an arrow sank deep into her eye. She screamed with pain
so loudly that even the sun was tempted to come out of
his hidingplace, but the thought of another arrow kept him
at bay. The moon wept and shook as she sank into a dense
cloud and she vowed that she would never appear again.

The hunter then turned his attention to the stars but
they were too dim to bother with. Besides, he needed some
light so that he could see how his plants were prospering.
Satisfied the hunter returned to his house, but he failed
to realize the damage he had done. The animals, the plants
and the people began to fall ill and the crops grew slowly,
if at all.

After their initial panic about the disappearance of the

sun and the moon, the creatures of the land and the air formed a council to discuss what to do.

The golden oriole opened the meeting. 'Who can suggest a way to invite the sun and the moon back to the sky?' she asked as she flew above the assembled crowd. She fluttered close to the animals and hovered above the ox's head. 'How about you?' she asked, 'Your deep lowing will surely be heard by the sun and he can pass your message on to the moon.'

The ox was pleased and proud to be chosen as the representative and he strolled to the front of the crowd. He took a position on the hillside where all the other animals and the sun would see him clearly.

'Mr Sun,' he called. 'It's safe for you to come out now. We want to see you again, so please come quickly.'

The sun heard the ox's deep lowing but decided not to come out, and so the ox called to him again. The sun continued to ignore his call. The ox repeated his reassurances eighteen times, but nothing would convince the sun to move from his safe spot.

'Perhaps his voice isn't strong enough,' cried a pig from the back of the crowd.

'Why don't we choose someone else? Perhaps the tiger would be willing to do it. He could call out to the moon. She might be listening,' suggested a dog at the front.

The tiger gave a yelp of delight, leaped to the front of the crowd and ran up the hillside to where the ox had been standing. He threw back his head and roared up to the moon. 'Miss Moon, come out soon, the sky is safe.'

The tiger's voice boomed across the sky and into the clouds but the moon was so frightened by the sound of it she did not dare show her face. The tiger tried again but finally lowered his head in regret. The council of animals admitted defeat and dispersed to their respective nests, lairs, caves and dens.

Three years later, when three-quarters of the earth's creatures had died from starvation, the animals convened another council. They sat in a circle mulling over the problem before them but, remembering that the proud tiger and the strong ox had failed in their previous attempts, they were unable to suggest anyone to follow these brave animals. When they had almost given up hope the cock strutted to the centre of the circle.

'Why don't you let me try? The sun is my cousin and I'm sure he will listen to me.'

'Yes, he could be right,' barked the dog. 'His voice is clear, he is related to the sun and we have nothing to lose if he fails to attract the sun's attention.'

Without waiting for agreement from the others, the cock tilted his head back and crowed as loud as he could. 'Cousin Sun, you have been hiding for far too long. There is nothing here to harm you any more. Come out and light our world again.'

The cock's voice rose to the heavens and woke the sun from his sleep. The sun edged himself out of the cloud and the cock called to him once more. The sun edged himself out even farther, accompanied by his cousin's encouragement, until his light flooded the heavens and the earth.

The sun was delighted to renew his acquaintance with the earth and its creatures, but he was surprised to discover that the shy moon was still hiding in the clouds. He danced across the sky and gently pushed her from the protective clouds.

'Today we will shine together,' he announced, 'and you will see that you have nothing to fear. When I rest tonight you will be safe to return to your old position in the sky.'

The sun then lowered himself in the sky and called out to the cock. 'I'm sure all that crowing must have exhausted you. Take this comb as a gift from me. You can use it to comb your fine feathers each morning.'

The sun threw a comb to the earth, but the cock was in such a rush to receive it that he ran forward and the comb landed upside down on his head with one end pointing towards the sun. Even today, the sun's present to the cock rests upside down on the cock's head.

Why the Sea is Salty

Thousands of years ago two brothers lived together close to the Eastern Sea. Ah Bong, the elder brother, was lazy and gluttonous, while Ah Dong, the younger brother, was hard-working, generous and easygoing. Ah Bong spent each day in bed, while his brother worked on the land and returned to cook the evening meal at sunset.

Early one morning Ah Dong left the house carrying a bundle of sticky rice for his lunch and headed for a nearby hill to cut some firewood. As he wielded his axe for the first time that morning an old dwarf jumped from behind the tree he was about to hack. Ah Dong lowered his axe and walked up to the dwarf to see if he could help him.

The old dwarf took Ah Dong's hand and gazed up at him with pleading eyes. 'I haven't eaten for days,' he moaned. 'Would you give me half of your lunch, please?'

It was difficult for Ah Dong to refuse the wizened dwarf, who looked as if he had not had a bath or a proper meal for at least a month. Ah Dong unwrapped the cabbage leaves around his sticky rice, divided the package into two and gave half to the dwarf. The dwarf grabbed it with his small gnarled fingers and pushed it into his mouth as quickly as he could. While his mouth was still bulging with food he licked his grubby fingers and demanded the other half of the sticky rice. Ah Dong hesitated for a moment because this was meant to sustain him until the evening, but the dwarf was so old and pitiful he did not have the heart to refuse him and so he handed over his remaining food. The dwarf ate this batch of sticky rice just as quickly and then he slumped against a tree burping and hiccuping with pleasure.

'You're a fine young man,' said the dwarf contentedly. 'I know few men who would give their last morsel of food to an absolute stranger. In return for your hospitality you must accept my gift.'

The dwarf drew out a well-worn stone box and cranked open its lid. He lifted out a small roughly-made stone grinder and handed it to Ah Dong.

'This is an extraordinary stone grinder,' said the dwarf proudly. 'All you have to do is ask it to grind and it will produce whatever you want, and when you want it to stop you just have to say, "Grinder, grinder, thank you very much" and it will stop immediately.'

Ah Dong accepted this original gift gratefully although he secretly doubted its declared powers. The dwarf then gave an elaborate bow of thanks and left Ah Dong to carry on with his work. Ah Dong placed the box carefully on a grassy patch of land and continued chopping wood. By noon he was hungry and so he decided to test the grinder. He held it gently in his hands and gave it the appropriate command.

'Grinder, grinder, please grind me a lump of sticky rice'.

His words miraculously set the grinder in motion and it churned out lump after lump of sticky rice. Ah Dong ordered the grinder to stop but it ignored him and bundles of rice continued to pour onto the floor. Eventually he remembered the polite command to stop.

'Grinder, grinder, thank you very much for your gifts. Now please stop.'

The grinder immediately halted its production and Ah Dong placed it respectfully back in its box. Afterwards he gathered up the lumps of sticky rice and put all except one in his straw sack. Their savoury smell was mouth-watering and they tasted better than any he had ever eaten before. The rice had been boiled to perfection and was laced with fruit, peanuts and peppers; just one lump gave him enough energy to work until sunset. In the evening he returned home laden with the rice, the grinder, his axe and a bag of wood.

Ah Bong had just woken up when his brother returned and he was busy rummaging in the kitchen cupboards for something to eat. He smelled the rice as soon as Ah Dong walked in the door. Without asking permission he grabbed the straw sack from his brother, ripped it apart and stuffed the rice into his mouth until he could not hold another grain. As he ate Ah Dong told him about the dwarf and the magic stone grinder.

While Ah Dong was still talking his brother grabbed the stone grinder, ran into the kitchen and ordered the stone to produce dinner. The grinder dutifully poured out dish after dish of delectable food. When Ah Bong was satisfied that he had enough he ordered the grinder to stop. But he forgot to ask it politely, so the grinder continued to pour out food. Just as Ah Bong began to panic his brother walked into the kitchen and, using the phrase the dwarf had taught him, asked the stone grinder to stop.

Throughout the meal Ah Bong had been suggesting ways that they could use the stone wisely but his brother said nothing until he had finished eating.

'Why do we have to be careful with this stone? It will give us anything. I know, let's use it to produce cartloads of fine salt. Who knows, if we sell enough we could be the richest men in China.'

'Let's discuss it in the morning,' said Ah Dong and went off to prepare their straw mattresses.

When Ah Dong had gone Ah Bong was still mulling over the various ways to make them rich. He finally decided not to share the future wealth with his brother. Ah Bong did not even bother to pack his bags – he just put the stone grinder under his arm and for the first time in months left the house. He ran down to the port where a merchant ship was ready to leave for southern China. He planned to travel to a secret place as far away from his brother as possible, a place where he would be wealthy and respected for the rest of his life.

After the anchor had been raised and the ship was heading for the open sea, Ah Bong placed the stone grinder on a quiet corner of the deck and demanded that the stone produce salt. The obedient stone began to churn out piles of salt, and Ah Bong knelt down beside it frantically shovelling the salt into hessian bags. The salt began to creep over the toes of his straw sandals and spread across the deck towards the galley. Ah Bong was afraid that someone might discover his secret so he ordered the grinder to stop, but the grinder took no notice. Again he commanded the grinder to stop, but it continued churning out piles of salt which now threatened to engulf the grinder itself.

Ah Bong had forgotten to say 'please' and 'thank you' and the grinder would not stop until these words had been spoken.

A creeping hill of salt made its way along the decks and down the stairs into the galley and although Ah Bong tried rephrasing his command he still forgot the most important words. Piles of salt now covered the grinder but still it kept on grinding. By now the crew had been alerted to the disaster and were desperately trying to shovel the salt overboard in case the boat sank, but they were no match for the dedicated grinder hidden away under a shifting mound of salt. The passengers began to panic and some jumped overboard in an attempt to swim for shore. Eventually even the crew abandoned ship. Only Ah Bong remained, determined to stay close to his precious stone grinder.

When the salt had reached Ah Bong's neck the boat began to sink and the sea water lashed across the deck. Within ten minutes the boat disappeared from sight beneath the waves. Ah Bong drowned but the grinder continued to produce salt, waiting for someone to tell it to stop.

It is still grinding away somewhere under the Eastern Sea, and that is why the sea tastes of salt.

The Dumb Flute Player

Ah Ch'in was dumb but when he played the flute those who heard him would stop whatever they were doing to listen to his perfect melodies. He would play for days and nights without stopping.

The people of the village had grown to love the dumb flute player but after five years of listening to the flute his wife had heard enough. One morning, after her husband had played for three days without end, she threw him out of the house and warned him not to come back until he had found himself a job.

The flute player was heartbroken and wandered down to the sea shore where he began to play a sad, haunting melody. The fish and the prawns were so entranced with his music that they floated to the surface to listen. Even the waves rolled to the shore in harmony with his notes. Within an hour the shore was littered with oysters, crabs, swordfish, jelly fish and every other creature of the ocean, basking in the soft notes that seemed to fill the air and the water.

Suddenly there was a commotion among the fish and

144

the waters of the ocean parted to reveal a path over the sea bed. In the distance the flute player saw a regiment of prawn and crab soldiers marching towards him and as they came closer he caught sight of the mighty Sea Dragon King at their head. The dumb flute player continued with his melody until the Sea Dragon King stood in front of him and raised his arm to command silence. He took the flute player by the arm and led him along the path between the waves.

'Your music is the most beautiful I have ever heard. The queen is ill, but even she felt better when she heard your melody,' said the Sea Dragon King as they approached the palace. 'Will you play each day in the palace so that my wife can recover?'

The flute player nodded in agreement and followed the king through the pearl gates of the palace. Since the queen had fallen ill the atmosphere in the palace had become heavy and foreboding, but as soon as the flute player began a melody the sadness that had penetrated every room lifted and the queen made a full recovery. As a reward the flute player was given the freedom of the palace and in time he became a trusted friend of the royal family.

The flute player's music was normally joyful but one evening the Sea Dragon King's attention was drawn to sad notes coming from the palace garden and he went in search of the flute player. He found the flute player leaning against a shady wall and as he played tears rolled down his face.

'What is wrong?' inquired the king. 'Are you lonely?'

The flute player nodded his head.

'Do you miss your home and family?' continued the king.

Once again the flute player nodded his head.

'Then I cannot keep you against your will,' replied the king. 'It saddens me to lose you but I will ask my crab guards to accompany you home. Before you go I want to give you this oyster which will open up and grant whatever you wish as soon as it hears your music.'

The king placed the oyster in the pocket of the flute player's silk robe and said his final goodbyes. Once again the sea parted and the flute player was led safely to the shore.

When the flute player returned to his home his wife welcomed him with caution but her attitude changed when she learned of the oyster's secret. Ah Chin placed the oyster on the kitchen table and started to play. The oyster danced across the table, leapt onto the floor and opened its shell wide in front of Ah Ch'in and his wife.

'Can you provide us with a banquet to welcome my husband home?' asked the wife tentatively and the oyster dutifully produced an abundance of succulent dishes.

'If this is your reward for playing the flute you can play for ever,' cried the wife.

The people of the village were now drawn to Ah Ch'in's house for there was the double attraction of his wonderful music and a fine array of food and whatever else Ah Ch'in or his friends needed.

When the cunning district magistrate heard of the precious oyster he was determined to have it and paid a courtesy visit to the flute player's house. Overwhelmed by the honour of the visit Ah Ch'in's wife asked the oyster to provide a banquet for his guest. When they had finished eating the district magistrate praised the qualities of the flute and the oyster at great length and offered to buy them from Ah Ch'in. The flute player's wife was afraid to disagree with the magistrate but Ah Ch'in shook his head violently in opposition. But the wily magistrate took his silence as agreement and promptly produced a pair of scales from his leather bag.

'As proof of my honesty I will exchange the oyster for the same weight in gold and silver,' he announced.

Ah Ch'in once again tried to stop the magistrate but the magistrate merely pushed him aside. He placed the oyster in one scale and three ingots of gold in the other, but the oyster was heavier. He added three ingots of silver, but the oyster still outweighed the money. The magistrate continued to pile precious metals and stones onto the scales, but nothing could raise the heavy oyster. In desperation the magistrate ordered his servants to bring a larger pair of scales. When this arrived he emptied the treasure and the oyster onto the new scales and continued to pile priceless gems on the lighter side.

By now a crowd had gathered and the magistrate was afraid to lose face so he continued to pour jewels onto the scales. The oyster remained obstinately on the lower side. When every bag of precious stone had been emptied the magistrate offered his official robe and his title to Ah Ch'in, for the oyster was worth far more to him than the money he could extort as a magistrate.

As soon as the magistrate placed his official hat and robe on the scales the oyster rose into the air and the scales balanced. With a sigh of relief the magistrate grabbed the oyster and the flute and ran to his house to test the oyster's magic. He locked the doors and the windows and before he began to play the flute he demanded that the oyster produce enough gold to fill his bedroom. The magistrate then raised the flute to his lips and began to play, but the notes were so loud and distorted that it made the passersby shudder. The magistrate continued undaunted, even though the oyster refused to open and the neighbours were banging against the walls in complaint. Eventually the oyster could not bear the din any longer and jumped onto the floor and hid itself in a cupboard.

The magistrate's screeching notes continued to ring through the village until the oyster jumped into the air in pain and cracked its shell on a wooden beam. The roof began to creak, the beams started to crack, the walls began to buckle, and while the magistrate wildly played the flute, his house fell around his shoulders. When the dust finally settled the magistrate crawled out of the remains of his shattered home, and although he searched for days he was unable to find the oyster.

Meanwhile Ah Ch'in was declared the new magistrate and with his newly acquired wealth he and his wife lived the life of immortals, but the cunning magistrate died a poor man.

The Pagoda Tree

Tung Yung lived with his crippled father in a small, mud house on the outskirts of a village. From the age of ten the boy had worked as a labourer to pay for the herbalist and the acupuncturist who regularly treated his father. When his father died Tung Yung was twenty years old and had spent all his earnings on medical care. He could not even afford to pay for his father's burial.

Tung Yung asked his friends and neighbours to lend him the money, but they all refused because they knew he could not repay his debts. Anxious to provide a grave for his father's body, he was driven to sell himself as a servant to a rich merchant called Liu. Liu provided the money for the burial and in return Tung Yung promised to work for three years in Liu's household. After burying his father Tung Yung made offerings to his ancestors. He left the graveyard with a sad heart for he knew he could not tend his father's grave or worship the ancestors for at least three years.

Tung Yung packed his few belongings in a sack and in the early hours of the morning headed for Liu's house on

149

the far side of the mountain. By noon he was halfway there and sat down under a tree to rest. He was suddenly startled by a girl's voice beside him.

'Are you Tung Yung?' she inquired.

Tung Yung was glad to hear a sympathetic voice and although he had never seen the woman before he introduced himself and told her the story of his father's death and his agreement with the merchant. By the time he had finished the story he had begun to cry.

'Don't be upset. I'll travel with you to the merchant's house and help you to cook, wash and clean. With me by your side the work will be done twice as fast and you can return home in less than three years.'

At first Tung Yung was ready to agree but he remembered that this strange woman had known his name and wondered if the gods were playing a trick. Even if she was a human being who had come to help him he could not arrive at the merchant's house with a strange girl at his side. But the girl read his thoughts and took him by the hand.

'If I agree to be your wife, will you marry me?' she asked him gently.

Tung Yung was dumbstruck and looked around desperately trying to think of an excuse.

'I can't, no, it's not right,' he spluttered. 'We can't marry without a matchmaker.'

The girl, unperturbed at his reply, walked to a large tree nearby and kicked its trunk. 'This is our matchmaker,' she replied calmly.

Tung Yung was now convinced she was either mad or an evil spirit, but to his astonishment the tree bent down as if to say yes. Tung Yung decided to humour her and asked her what good this matchmaker would be if it could only nod but not speak.

'Who says I can't speak!' cried an indignant, throaty voice from the tree behind him. 'I'm your matchmaker and I order you to marry.'

By now Tung Yung was convinced that good or evil spirits were at work and he bowed down to their forces and took the girl as his wife.

When the couple arrived at Liu's house they were led to his reception room. Liu was furious to discover that he had another mouth to feed, but the girl reassured him that she could sew, weave and clean faster than any servant in the house. The crafty merchant considered her words and agreed to let her stay on the condition that she could weave twenty-four pieces of cloth in three days. On hearing this Tung Yung demanded to know how his wife could fulfil this condition, but all she would say was, 'Don't worry, weaving is easy for me.'

Three days later the weaving was completed and she laid the pieces of cloth in front of Liu. While the merchant examined them with an air of disdain, Tung Yung hugged his wife with joy. During the three days, he had not seen her weave one thread and yet she had completed the task.

'You have my permission to stay,' said Liu haughtily, 'but don't expect me to give you free food. Unless you can weave fifty pieces of fine silk in three days you will be thrown out of this house.'

When his master had left the room Tung Yung fell to his knees in despair. 'How can he expect you to weave fifty pieces of silk in three days? This is the end. I know I'll never see you again.'

But once again Tung Yung's wife reassured him that she would complete the work in time.

During the next two days Tung Yung watched his wife carefully. She spent her time picking flowers in the garden but never once did she enter the weaving room. Even the merchant was surprised to see her acting so casually and looked forward to throwing her out of his household.

On the evening of the second day Tung Yung was so worried he could not sleep. Instead he crept to the weaving room to see if his wife had begun her task. He pushed the door open slightly and peered into the brightly lit room. He saw a white crane drop a weaving shuttle into his wife's hand and in turn she threw the shuttle to the weaving machine and the machine began to weave quickly without anyone's help. Tung Yung rubbed his eyes, convinced that this was all a dream, and when he opened them again the crane and his wife had disappeared and the weaving room was dark. Convinced he had been dreaming, Tung Yung returned to bed.

At daybreak on the third day the girl laid fifty pieces of finely woven silk before Liu. 'I am sure you will find the right amount of silk here,' she said, and she bowed and left the room.

Liu was so surprised he spent the whole morning marvelling at her skill. In the late afternoon he summoned her to his reception room.

'Can you embroider silk?' he demanded.

The girl nodded.

'In that case I want you to weave and embroider fifty pieces of silk in ten days. If you can do that I will sell the silk and buy fifty slaves and in return you and your husband will be free to leave. If you fail you will have to stay with me for six years instead of three.'

The merchant was sure that the girl could not complete this task and he rubbed his beard in anticipation of the money he would make if she stayed in his service for six years.

During the next ten days Tung Yung was unable to sleep or eat. He saw his wife resting in the gardens each day and imagined how overgrown his father's grave would be in six year's time. Each time he reproached his wife she brushed him aside, so by the ninth night Tung Yung was almost frantic with worry.

At midnight on the ninth night Tung Yung was pacing up and down his room when he heard women's voices coming from the weaving room. He approached and cautiously opened the door. He was rooted to the spot in amazement by what he saw. His wife and six beautiful girls were weaving and embroidering perfect pieces of silk. Seven cranes flew above their heads handing them shuttles and fine-coloured silk embroidery threads. Tung Yung was too exhausted to cope with this shock and he collapsed in the doorway.

When Tung Yung awoke his wife was bathing his forehead and trying to placate him.

'I'm sorry to shock you like that but it was only my six older sisters who came to help me weave the silk. Now it's finished and we're free to leave.'

At the appointed time on the tenth day the girl laid fifty pieces of silk, finely embroidered with dragons, ducks and phoenix, before her master. Liu was speechless with surprise and, realizing he had no power over this girl or her husband, he dismissed them from his sight.

Tung Yung and his wife began the journey across the mountain that afternoon, but the girl insisted on stopping by the tree where they had first met. Tung Yung ran to the tree and hugged it with joy, but there was no response from the tree, and when he turned to his wife to tell her she opened her straw bag and handed him ten perfect rolls of silk.

'This is my parting gift to you,' she explained. 'I am an immortal and I took human shape to help you, but the Jade Emperor has learned of our marriage and I am forced to go back to Heaven. Take this silk, sell it in the market and use the money that you earn wisely. I will always take care of you.'

Tung Yung tried to kiss her goodbye but she rose towards the clouds before he could touch her. He gazed up and saw her flying to Heaven surrounded by seven cranes.

Why the Earthworm has no Eyes

At one time the earthworm had eyes so he could see. He could also swim and move quickly over the ground. The earthworm's closest friend was the prawn and although the prawn had no eyes the earthworm helped him swim and walk on dry land.

The earthworm enjoyed swimming but each time he went in the water he was bullied and insulted by the crab general. One day the crab general tried to drown him but he escaped to his burrow, where he sat crying with fear and shock. When the prawn discovered his friend in tears he asked him how he could help.

'One day the crab general will kill me because I am too weak and soft to defend myself,' the earthworm replied. 'But you have a strong body, a stout helmet and a protective coat. I will lend you my eyes if you will help me exact revenge on the crab general. But once you have finished, will you give me back my eyes?'

The prawn agreed to help his friend and watched while the earthworm screeched and wriggled as he pulled out his eyes. The prawn received the eyes, placed one on either side of his nose and set off full of courage to fight the crab general. He swam along the water's edge calling to the crab general, but when his adversary loomed into sight the prawn was so frightened by this dangerous-looking creature that he ran away and hid in the rocks under the water. When the coast was clear the prawn emerged from his hiding place. He was enjoying his new eyes so much that he decided not to return them.

Even though the prawn had legs, from that time he no longer dared to walk on dry land in case the earthworm asked for his eyes back. Meanwhile the poor earthworm is still waiting for his friend to return. Even though he has lost his eyes he can still swim, but he is too afraid to go into the water in case he is murdered by the crab general.

The Loud-Mouthed Woman

The god of Hell was in charge of all the ghosts who lived in the underworld, but it was a boring, monotonous job. Hell was cool and dark and they rarely had any visitors. In desperation the god of Hell went to see the Judge of the Dead and begged him to change more human beings into ghosts so that his life in Hell would be busier and more enjoyable.

The Judge of the Dead agreed with the god of Hell and so they sent their most devious ghost to earth to kill as many people as possible. The ghost stopped first at the farm of a woman called Wong Fu. While she was cooking in the kitchen he crept into her chicken coop and released all her fowl. When Wong Fu saw her birds flying in all directions across the farmyard she chased after them but the birds were not willing to give up their freedom and with the help of the ghost they always kept one step ahead of her. Eventually Wong Fu collapsed and died of a heart attack. The devious ghost escorted her to the Judge of the Dead and she was sent to Hell.

The ghost then returned to earth and arrived at the

home of a rich man who spent every afternoon counting his money. The ghost crept up beside him and started to throw his gold and silver coins out of the window onto the heads of the passers-by. The rich man desperately tried to hold on to his coins but they slid out of his hands like oily fish. When all his money had disappeared the rich man fell into his chair, clutching his heart and died. He too was escorted down to Hell.

The devious ghost was pleased with his success and continued to frighten and harass people whenever and wherever he could. Sometimes he only had to show his ugly black face and yellow fangs to cause immediate death from shock. After a week the rooms of Hell were bustling with new ghosts and the god of Hell had begun to smile again.

The wily ghost was given one more week to find new members before he returned to Hell and so he was determined to kill even more people than he had the previous week.

One morning, as he was travelling through the country-side he smelled the mouth-watering aroma of hot lard. He tracked the source to a house where a woman was preparing lunch for her family. The woman was tall, strong, and bony, and she was known locally as 'the loud-mouthed woman'. When the ghost spotted her she was just about to pour the lard into an earthenware jar, so he ran to catch a mouthful, but he arrived just as the jar was being sealed. He stamped his foot in annoyance.

'She is a selfish loud-mouthed woman,' he grumbled to himself, 'and as a punishment I'm going to spray hot oil in her face so she will die of burns.'

As the ghost prepared to throw a jar of oil at the woman a boy ran into the house with his face covered in mud.

'Look at your filthy black face,' cried the woman. 'I've warned you a thousand times not to play in the mud.'

When the little boy began to cry the woman softened

and added jokingly, 'I'm going to boil a pot of water and boil you in it till every pore of your body is cleaned.'

When the ghost heard this he thought the woman was speaking to him and he quivered with fear. He was not afraid of anything except water and, without a second glance at the woman, he dropped his pot of oil and ran back to Hell. He breathlessly told the Judge of the Dead about his female rival who had threatened to boil him in water. The Judge listened patiently to the ghost's story and then sent him back to Hell for a rest. He decided to visit this loud-mouthed woman himself to see if she really was so dangerous.

When the Judge of the Dead arrived at the loud-mouthed woman's house he changed himself into a wooden log and lay right across the threshold of her front door. He called her name and she came running, but she stopped abruptly when she saw the log and demanded to know who had left it in this dangerous place. There was nobody around to listen to her complaints and so she summoned her husband. The Judge of the Dead quivered when he heard her penetrating voice and the husband obediently came running when he heard his wife's call.

'Chop this wood immediately,' she demanded, 'so that we can have cooking fuel for tonight's meal.' She kicked the log of wood out of the way and hurried back into the kitchen.

While her husband went to fetch an axe the Judge of the Dead changed back into his normal form and rubbed his bruised body. Before the woman had a chance to hurt him again he flew back to Hell where he reported the story to the god of Hell. The god of Hell had already heard of this woman from his most devious ghost and was amused to discover that even the Judge of the Dead had trouble with her.

'I don't know what's got into you,' said the god of Hell with a wry smile. 'From your reports I imagine this woman to have three heads and six arms. I have to see her for myself. I'm sure I'll bring her to Hell within the day.'

It was sunset when the god of Hell arrived on the earth and he changed into a shadow so that he could glide silently through the loud-mouthed woman's house. The family was gathered in the kitchen in readiness for their evening meal and he looked around for a safe place to hide. There was a large earthenware jar full of snails standing in the shadows in the corner of the kitchen, so the god of Hell changed himself into a fat snail and settled in the jar. While he was mulling over the various ways he could kill the woman he heard her ask her son to collect a bowl of the fattest snails he could find from the earthenware jar. The god of Hell saw the child's hand feeling the snails around him and hauling out the juiciest ones. Several times the child's fingers brushed his body but he wriggled deeper and deeper into the mass of snails. Finally the child's hand disappeared and the god of Hell fled back home, feeling lucky to have escaped with his life.

The god of Hell was still breathless and shaken when he reported back to the devious ghost and the Judge of the Dead.

'Now I know what you mean,' he exclaimed, 'I consider myself fortunate to be back in Hell. I think she's the sort of woman who is best left alone.'

The Judge of the Dead agreed with this assessment, but the devious ghost was even more determined to kill the loud-mouthed woman. When no one was looking, he slipped back to earth and entered her house. He grabbed her unfortunate husband, gagged him, locked him in the woodshed and took his shape. In this new disguise he climbed into the couple's bed and waited for the loud-mouthed woman to come to bed. He waited and waited, but the woman did not enter the room, and eventually he was forced to go and look for her. He found her washing her feet in the kitchen. The devious ghost crept up behind her, put his hands on her shoulders and spoke to her in his most appealing voice.

'Why don't you let me wash you? You're tired and you've been working hard. I'll rub oil into your skin to soften it.'

He felt the loud-mouthed woman's shoulders quiver but instead of turning to him with a smile she seized the bucket, swung round, and threw the water over him. Then she marched out of the kitchen, slamming the door behind her. The devious ghost gave a deathly scream as his body began to melt, but the god of Hell heard his piercing cry and sent two ghosts to carry him back to Hell.

When the devious ghost had recovered he and all the other ghosts in Hell were summoned to a meeting by the god of Hell.

'I have had enough,' he declared. 'That woman is to be left alone. I don't want to listen to her voice for eternity and if there are others like her it is best to avoid the human world altogether.'

Everyone agreed with the god of Hell, and from that moment on, the ghosts and the Judge of the Dead never bothered human beings again.

Ma Chen and the Immortal Brush Pen

Ma Chen was a fifteen-year-old orphan who made a living as a labourer and gardener. In his spare time he liked to draw but he could not afford a pen or parchment and so he drew in the sand with a small branch.

One night an old man appeared in Ma Chen's dreams holding a brush pen. He bent over Ma Chen's bed and touched the boy's forehead with the pen. 'This is an immortal brush pen,' he said gently.

The tip of the pen was so bright that it lit the whole house, but when Ma Chen sat up in bed to thank the old man, he had disappeared. At that moment Ma Chen awoke and discovered that he was holding the pen the old man had given him in his dream. Ma Chen ran out of his house and by the light of an oil lamp he drew a bird in the sand. As he put the final touches to the bird's wings the bird shook its feathers and flew away into the darkness. Ma Chen drew a fish and as soon as the picture was finished the fish wriggled in the sand and then jumped in to a nearby stream.

Ma Chen discovered that he could draw anything. As

long as he completed the picture it would come to life in front of him. He used his skill to help those in need in his village. If his neighbour needed a hoe to work the land, he would draw a hoe; if his neighbour needed an oil lamp Ma Chen would produce it. The orphan would even produce medicinal herbs for those who were too poor to pay the herbalist. The poor of the village loved him and he became famous in the area as Immortal Brush Pen Ma Chen.

When a local wealthy landowner heard of this magic pen he ordered his servants to bring Ma Chen to his house. But Ma Chen knew that the avaricious landowner wanted to abuse his skills and so he refused to draw. As a punishment he was thrown in the stables and locked in without food or blankets until he changed his mind.

But Ma Chen still had his pen hidden inside his shirt. He drew a stove and some pastries and brought them to life so that he could eat.

When the delicious aroma wafted into the landowner's dining room, he ordered the servants to snatch the pen from the boy. Ten servants rushed into the stable but Ma Chen had climbed up a ladder onto the roof. When the servants jumped on the ladder it disappeared beneath their feet and they fell in a heap on the floor. By the time they had recovered from their fall Ma Chen had disappeared.

The orphan ran for days and nights on end until he reached a town that reminded him of his own town far away. He settled down in a hut not far from the market-place and spent his days drawing pictures in the sand. Everybody stopped on their way to or from the market to admire his skill, but Ma Chen was careful never to complete any pictures in case they came to life and his identity was discovered. If he drew a man, the man's hand or foot was always missing; if he drew a bird, the eyes were always missing; and if he drew a house, the doors were always missing.

One morning as Ma Chen drew a crane a large crowd

of people gathered around his hut. As he turned to thank them for their praise he accidently dropped two spots of black ink on the bird's head. The crane came to life and flew away. Ma Chen's secret had been discovered and before long he was summoned to the Emperor.

Ma Chen was loathe to draw for the greedy Emperor, so when he was commanded to draw a dragon he drew a snake which writhed and spat at the Emperor. When he was commanded to draw a phoenix he drew a jet-black crow which flew above the Emporer and defecated on his head.

By now the Emperor was tired of the orphan's tricks and he snatched the pen from Ma Chen to create his own pictures. The Emperor drew a mountain of rubies, jade, cornelians, amber, diamonds and crystal. He continued to draw until the pile of precious stones was higher than his throne. When he had finally created enough wealth the Emperor tossed the brush aside and threw himself onto the stones. Then he let out a piercing cry of disgust for the moment he touched the stones they changed into a pile of animal excreta.

The Emperor could hardly breathe and struggled wildly to escape, cursing Ma Chen every time he managed to gasp a mouthful of air. His guards tied scarves around their noses and mouths to keep out the foul stench and hauled the Emperor out of the excreta. It took four days for the Emperor to rid himself of the smell, which had sunk into his skin. When he had finally recovered he again summoned Ma Chen to the throneroom.

'This time,' said the Emperor, 'I will let you draw something that is pleasing to the eye. Draw me a sea view that I can sit back and enjoy when I am bored.'

Ma Chen was desperate to leave the palace and so he did as he was commanded and drew a calm sea. The Emperor was pleased and demanded fishes, so Ma Chen drew hundreds of fishes of all shapes and sizes to fill the sea. The Emperor was still not content and wanted a boat, so Ma Chen drew a large wooden boat bobbing on the water. The Emperor was delighted and jumped into the boat, but now he wanted a wind to drive the boat. Again Ma Chen did as he was told. But the Emperor wanted more wind, and so the orphan painted five black strokes of wind on the sea. But the strokes of paint were too strong and they changed into a gale and torrential rain which tossed the boat until it almost sank. The Emperor clung to the mast and screeched for help, so Ma Chen drew a large sun in the sky to calm the storm. Then before anyone could stop him, he ran for his life from the palace.

When Ma Chen disappeared the storm and the sea also disappeared and the Emperor found himself lying in a pool of water beside his throne. Afraid that Ma Chen had the power to destroy his authority, the Emperor allowed the orphan to live and travel in peace throughout the kingdom. From that time on the wealthy were afraid of Ma Chen and he worked only among the poor in the villages and towns of China.

The Mad Monk

Many years ago there was a farmer called T'an Ta Hu who lived in the Hangchow area of Chehkiang. For many years he had been plagued by a strange illness that caused his stomach to bulge. Sometimes it was so swollen he could not stand up. Over the years his mother, T'an Ta Liang, had experimented with every known medicinal herb but nothing would cure her son. One day a travelling salesman visited the house and recommended that she visit Chi Kung, a strange monk who lived alone in Ling Yin Temple near the Western Lake of Chehkiang. He told her many stories of the monk's supernatural healing powers and recounted in vivid detail how he saw a blind man healed in less than a minute, a hump-backed woman stand straight for the first time in forty years, and a broken leg healed the moment ointment was rubbed on the fractured part. The travelling salesman continued with his tales until T'an Ta Liang was convinced that this monk could cure her son.

Although T'an Ta Liang was old she made the two-day journey to Ling Yin Mountain alone and climbed up the rocky slopes to Ling Yin Temple, perched on the top of the mountain. The temple was dilapidated and damp but after searching amongst the many rooms she came across Chi Kung slumped against a pillar, dozing and muttering to himself. Even though she kept her distance from the monk, every time he breathed out she was overcome by strong fumes of wine. While he dozed she noticed that his red robe was ripped and stained, his hat was torn and his straw sandals were threadbare. His face was dirty, and one leg was covered with suppurating boils. By his side lay a rush leaf fan and from time to time he would use it to brush away the flies that landed on his sores. T'an Ta Liang was so worried for her son that she didn't care how disgusting or dirty the monk looked and she fell to her knees beside him.

'Human immortal, please help me,' she begged, but the monk only grunted in reply and turned on his side. She continued to beg and plead for more than an hour until he eventually came to his senses and looked at her with bleary eyes. T'an Ta Liang poured out the story of her son while the monk sat burping and muttering to himself. When she had finally finished her tearful story Chi Kung yawned and rubbed his hand across his corpulent stomach. He continued to rub his dirty flesh until he had formed two small pellets of dirt which he placed in the palm of his hand and offered to T'an Ta Liang. The old woman recoiled in disgust.

'Don't be shocked. Only these pellets can heal your son,' said the monk. 'Take them home and try them.' He handed the pellets to her, yawned, and fell asleep again.

T'an Ta Liang placed the pellets in her skirts and left the sleeping monk. When she arrived home and presented the two balls of dirt to her son he refused to swallow them but she forced them down his throat. T'an Ta Hu felt the pellets slowly slide into his stomach, settle against his stomach wall and then erupt. He felt as though his stomach was on fire and he fell into a convulsion before he was violently sick on the floor. He vomited a nest of water tics which had been living in his stomach since he was a child. T'an Ta Hu eventually collapsed on the floor but when he awoke several hours later he was completely cured.

Ta'n Ta Liang was overjoyed at her son's recovery and spread the word amongst the neighbourhood of a living Buddha working in Ling Yin Temple. Although many people came to visit Chi Kung he still behaved like a mad beggar, drinking heavily, and eating anything he could lay his hands on.

One day Chi Kung approached the straw hut of a young boy selling sweet and savoury buns to support his crippled mother. The boy rarely left his hut and had never heard of the 'living Buddha'.

Chi Kung staggered up to the boy and sniffed the air with pleasure. 'What a wonderful smell,' he announced. 'I want to buy ten of your buns.'

'Whatever you want,' replied the boy as he bowed respectfully to Chi Kung.

The boy lifted the lid of his steamer and showed the monk his selection. Without being asked, Chi Kung immersed his dirty hand in the pan and fingered every bun before he selected ten meat ones. The boy placed the buns in a small straw bag and handed them to the monk. Chi Kung bit into one but immediately spat it out in disgust.

'I'm not eating this,' he spluttered, his mouth full of food, 'There's too much fat in it. Give me ten vegetable buns instead.'

The boy obediently did as the monk demanded and handed over the vegetable buns.

Again Chi Kung took a mouthful and spat it out. 'This is rubbish!' he cried, 'Give me something with some meat in it.'

The monk pushed the boy aside and once again fingered every bun in the steamer until he had selected ten meat buns that were satisfactory. Chi Kung then pushed a whole bun into his mouth, squeezed the other nine into the pocket of his robe and wandered off down the road.

'Wait! You haven't paid for anything!' cried the boy. But the monk ignored him and carried on walking. 'Wait! Don't go!' cried the boy, and he ran down the road after Chi Kung.

When the boy finally caught up with Chi Kung and demanded payment the monk merely raised his arms in surprise. 'But I don't owe you any money,' he said, spitting food into the boy's face as he spoke. 'I exchanged ten vegetable buns for ten meat buns.'

'But you didn't pay for the vegetable buns,' replied the boy angrily.

'No, I didn't. That's because I exchanged the vegetable buns for meat buns,' replied the monk irritably.

The monk's replies confused the boy and while he stood pondering their logic Chi Kung waddled quickly down the road. When the boy realized that he was escaping he chased after him and as he ran he heard a roll of thunder come from the mountain behind him. He swung round to catch sight of his hut being demolished by an avalanche of boulders that hit the ground with such force that the earth reverberated. It was only then that the boy realized the monk had saved his life by refusing to pay for the buns. When he turned round to thank Chi Kung the monk was asleep under a tree and at his side lay two half-eaten buns covered in saliva.

Chi Kung opened one eye at the boy's approach and pointed to the buns. 'Take these and give them to your mother. Don't waste your time here,' he said, eager to return to his sleep.

Once again Chi Kung's remedy worked and as soon as she had eaten the buns the boy's mother was cured. When she heard her son's story she knew that they had been saved by one of the immortals, and for the rest of her life she made daily offerings to Heaven.

The Min River

More then two thousand years ago a bad-tempered river god made his home in the Min River. Whenever he felt cross he created floods that demolished all the houses round about and if he was particularly angry he would kill any humans who strayed near the river. The local people learned to placate the river god with animal sacrifice and for a long time he was content to receive one cow and one sheep every week.

One day he rose from the waters and, with a mighty roar, demanded that the villagers provide him with a beautiful girl. The local people hurriedly found the prettiest girl in the area, provided her with an extensive dowry and sent her down to the river. The river god accepted the gift and promised to remain calm, but after two years of peace he lost his temper and ruined the village harvest with a flood.

Not long after this disaster a new prefect called Li Ping was posted to the village. Within a day of his arrival he had received more than fifty complaints about the river

god and was shocked to discover that the whole village
lived in fear of the bad-tempered god.

The following morning Li Ping fastened his official
white jade belt around his waist and set off for the river
to negotiate with the god. An eager and respectful crowd
followed him down to the river bank and crowded into the
river god's temple. They watched with bated breath as Li
Ping held a goblet of wine up to the altar and fearlessly
introduced himself to the god. As Li Ping raised the goblet
to his lips a slight wind blew through the temple. The
crowd began to edge back and a murmur passed through
the crowd that the river god was arriving. The wind
increased, the waters started to rise, the sky grew dark
and the candles and joss sticks were extinguished. The
villagers hid in fear behind the pillars of the temple. The
only thing that could be seen was the prefect's brilliant
white jade belt.

Suddenly the wind dropped, the sun returned to the
sky and the waters calmed down. The prefect still stood
undaunted before the altar and the crowd let out a cheer
of admiration for the man who had the courage to face
the river god. Only the prefect realized that the river god
was still with them for the wine in the goblet was still
moving. Li Ping calmed the excited crowd and raised his
voice to the river god.

'God of the Min river, I've brought the people of the
village to talk to you. They want to be reassured that you
will never break your promise again. Surely you have the
power and the wisdom to see how much these people
suffer when you create a flood?'

When Li Ping had finished speaking the wine cup was
lifted from his hands by an invisible force and thrown to
the ground. The goblet shattered on the stone floor and
the prefect disappeared.

The crowd began to panic and jostled with each other
to squeeze through the narrow door of the temple and
escape to their homes. But as they ran along the river path

back to the village they were confronted by the sight of two green rhinoceros fighting on the river bank. The animals' horns were locked in battle and neither could force the other to surrender. The grassy spot where they were fighting had been churned into mud and they pushed each other with all their might in one direction and then in another. One rhinoceros managed to disentangle his horns and ran into the river but he was pursued by his opponent. Both animals then disappeared beneath the surface and the river was calm. The villagers were too frightened to investigate the murky waters of the river, and so they continued on their way.

As they approached the village Li Ping came running towards them, dripping in water.

'I need your help,' he panted. 'The river god has tremendous power and can change form at will. You have just seen us fighting but my power is limited so if the river god attacks me again you must kill him. But be careful not to shoot me by mistake for we are identical in appearance. If you look closely you will see that I am wearing a white jade belt around my right hind leg.'

Li Ping had barely finished speaking when a rhinoceros rose from the water and galloped furiously towards the crowd. Li Ping immediately changed shape while the guards raised their arrows and the two mighty animals were once again engaged in combat. The animals flung each other on the floor and their bodies were so entangled it was difficult to make out which was which. Soon one of the rhinoceros began to weaken and the stronger one began to gore it with its horns. The guards now identified the river god and pierced his thick skin with a barrage of arrows. The god changed back to his old shape and tried to crawl back to the river but he died at the water's edge.

From that day the waters of the Min river have never flooded and the spot where the river god and the prefect fought is still known as the Fighting Rhinoceros Terrace.

Ting Ling Goddess

Seventeen hundred years ago, at the time of the Three
States, a childless couple lived in the town of Hai Ling in
Kiangsu province. They had tried to have children for
many years and then, when they had given up hope, the
woman conceived and gave birth to a girl. They treated
her as a gift from Heaven and called her their 'Precious
Pearl'.

The people of the village remarked on the good fortune
of the couple because they had a girl who was more
intelligent, kind and generous than any other child in the
village. As she grew older the matchmaker regularly visited
her house with proposals of marriage, but the girl refused
every offer, explaining that her parents were old and
needed her to help them.

One winter, when the weather was bitterly cold, her
parents caught pneumonia and as the winter progressed
their condition got worse. Just as the girl was sure they
were going to die, a skilled Taoist priest called Liu Kang
passed through the town. He stopped at her house and
asked for food and water. While the girl drew water from

172

the well and prepared a bowl of rice, the Taoist priest watched her attentively. He knew by her movements and her character that she had the strength and the spirit to be his student. By the time he had finished eating he had offered himself as her teacher and she had accepted. The girl proved an astute student; the speed with which she learned Taoist magic surprised even the priest. Within a week she had become adept at Taoist practices and as her skill increased so did her parents' health. Within a month her parents had made a full recovery and she had acquired the skill to practise her magic to good effect among the people of the village.

After two years Liu Kang had taught her everything he knew, and he left her to practise her magic wisely. But before he departed he gave her the title Ting Ling Goddess.

A month after the Taoist priest had left a poor man called Ah Tu passed through Hai Ling and stopped by chance outside Ting Ling's house to beg for food. Ah Tu was a polite and educated man and he explained to the family that he had been robbed by bandits over a year ago and had been forced to beg for food and shelter ever since. Out of pity, Ting Ling's parents asked him to stay, and before long they had summoned the matchmaker to arrange the marriage between Ah Tu and their daughter. Ting Ling unwillingly agreed to her parent's wishes on the condition that she could still practise her magic.

Ting Ling had the power to appear and disappear at will and at least twice a day she would suddenly disappear to practise her magic somewhere in the province and then, just as suddenly she would return. Ah Tu always demanded an explanation from his wife but she refused to say where she had been or what she had been doing.

When Ting Ling was at home the house was always full of people requesting help and as the months wore on Ah Tu became jealous of his wife's popularity. If people came to call he told them that his wife was too busy to see them, but Ting Ling also had the power to see and hear at great distances and would always reappear just as her husband said this.

Eventually Ah Tu became so exasperated with his wife's behaviour that he locked her in the bedroom, saying that no one should see her, but the moment he locked the door she used her magic to pass through the bedroom wall and to travel into town.

When Ah Tu realized that he had no control over his wife's movements he began to beat her until her body was covered in bruises which even her skilled Taoist magic could not hide. The people of the town cursed the man who had harmed Ting Ling.

Two years after their marriage Ah Tu went to the district magistrate and accused his wife of evil magic. He claimed that his wife's Taoist skills were proof of her sorcery and the magistrate had no choice but to arrest and imprison her. Ting Ling could not prove her innocence as any magical feat would only be misinterpreted as evil power.

While Ting Ling spent her days meditating in prison her parents fell ill with grief. They regretted the day they had ever opened their doors to Ah Tu.

The people of the province turned against Ting Ling but her friends and neighbours in Hai Ling remained loyal. Ah Tu refused to feed his wife's parents and spent the family money gambling and drinking with the beggars and strangers who passed through the town. He left his house only under cover of darkness because his neighbours threw stones and spat at him whenever he appeared. When all his money was spent Ah Tu abandoned his parents-in-law and secretly left Hai Ling, vowing never to return.

Meanwhile the prison guards had received orders not to feed Ting Ling in the hope that the evil spirit would be forced out of her body. She relied solely on food smuggled into the prison by her friends. From a note hidden in a rice cake she learned of her husband's departure and her parents' imminent death. From that moment she prepared to leave her body but retain her spirit. She began by refusing to eat. Each day she went into a deep trance; nothing the guards said or did could wake her from her dream-like state.

One morning the guards entered her cell with a jug of water but Ting Ling was no longer there. Their attention was drawn to a rustling sound from the cell window and they turned to catch sight of a green bird disappearing through the iron bars.

Ting Ling had left her body for ever but her spirit was immortal. Several days after her escape her parents died peacefully and the neighbours reported the sight of a green bird hovering around the house. In the following weeks whenever someone recovered from an illness or a criminal was arrested, many people claimed to have seen a green bird nearby. Slowly the people of the province realized that Ting Ling was still with them and always would be.

A temple was built in her honour on a mountainside outside Hai Ling and the green bird made her nest in one of its walls. Ting Ling rested there each night, but whenever she was needed she would travel across the province at great speed. She was reported in a hundred different places at once and nobody dared to commit an offence because they knew she would hover above the scene of the crime. And that is why Kiangsu province was the safest place to live during the time of the Three States.

The Little Fox
and the Pomegranate King

Mu Tai was a poor man who lived alone on the outskirts of a town called Hsin Chiang. The only thing that survived on the small patch of land beside his hut was a pomegranate tree which bore succulent fruit. He loved the tree and talked to it as though it were a child, scolding it if its blossom were late and praising it when it bore fruit.

Mu Tai counted the number of pomegranates on his tree each day and one autumn he discovered that two disappeared each evening. He decided to stay awake throughout the night to find out who was stealing his fruit. One night when the moon was full he caught sight of a fox rummaging in the branches of the pomegranate tree. The following evening he poured a circle of transparent glue around the base of the tree and went to bed. In the morning the fox was glued to the base of the tree yelping with pain as he desperately tried to free his paws. Mu Tai grabbed the fox by its ears and threatened to kill him, but the wily animal was prepared to make an offer that Mu Tai could not refuse.

'If you free me I promise to find a princess to marry you,' said the fox confidently. But Mu Tai shook the fox in disbelief. 'Please believe me,' continued the fox, 'I swear to you by the end of the month you will be the son-in-law of an emperor.'

Mu Tai was tempted by the fox's offer and so he freed him from the glue and gave him a week's reprieve to fulfil his promise. The fox slunk away to his den to devise a plan.

Several days later the fox stole a guard's uniform, put it on, brushed his tail and set off to visit an old emperor who ruled a nearby kingdom. By his powers of persuasion the fox gained access to the Emperor and introduced himself as the chief guard and adviser to Emperor Mu Tai. He told the gullible emperor how he had seen thousands of pearls, cornelians and rubies scattered in the soil of Mu Tai's palace gardens and he wished to borrow a sieve from the neighbouring kingdom. The old Emperor was impressed by the fox's appearance and rhetoric and offered him a large oak sieve.

That night the fox crept into the old Emperor's palace and stole a handful of pearls from the treasury. Two days later he returned to the palace and placed the sieve on the floor in front of the Emperor. As he did so he deliberately dropped eight pearls into the sieve. When the palace servants placed the sieve in the Emperor's hands the pearls rolled into his lap. The Emperor was duly impressed with their translucent quality and the fox offered them as a gift.

'I have plenty more,' said the fox proudly. 'These pearls are so small compared with the others that I failed to notice them.'

The Emperor pondered on the fox's words for a few minutes and then he whispered to a minister of the court who stood by his side. Finally the Emperor came down from the throne and took the fox to one side.

'I'm growing old and I'm quite concerned about my unmarried daughter,' said the Emperor confidentially. 'Would you accept the role of matchmaker between my daughter and your Emperor?'

The fox agreed with pleasure and reassured the Emperor that Emperor Mu Tai would make a perfect match for his daughter. He promised to return for the marriage ceremony the following week and left with a flourishing bow and a sweep of his tail.

Mu Tai received the fox's news with a mixture of delight and worry. He had no possessions to offer the princess; he did not even have a suit of clothes or a pair of shoes. The fox reassured Mu Tai that all would be well and ordered him to be ready for their departure to the neighbouring kingdom in a week's time.

A week later the fox arrived at Mu Tai's house carrying a blanket and he led the nervous groom to the old emperor's palace. Just before they reached the palace gates the fox ordered Mu Tai to jump in a lake. Mu Tai did as the fox commanded, and when he emerged from the freezing water the fox threw away Mu Tai's torn clothes and wrapped him in the blanket. When this was done they marched into the palace and presented themselves to the emperor.

'Your Majesty, I bring you Emperor Mu Tai,' announced the fox proudly as Mu Tai stood half-naked and shivering in front of the Emperor. We have suffered the most incredible misfortune. We were on our way to your kingdom with forty camels loaded with silks and precious stones, but when we tried to cross the river outside your palace the narrow bridge collapsed, the camels were drowned, the marriage gifts were carried away by the current and we were lucky to escape with our lives.'

The Emperor was impressed by the thought of forty camels laden with precious goods and ordered his dressers to clothe Mu Tai in the finest robes. That evening Mu Tai and the princess were married and celebrated their union at a magnificent banquet. But Mu Tai was so worried he could barely eat and, when no one was listening, he confronted the fox.

'It's all very well to be married to a princess and to be addressed as Emperor, but what will happen when she comes to my home and discovers my poverty?'

The fox brushed Mu Tai's worries aside and told him to enjoy this unaccustomed splendour.

Early the following morning, when the banquet was over, the newly married couple left the palace for Mu Tai's home, accompanied by a caravan of horses, donkeys and carts laden with the princess's servants and dowry. Mu Tai was once again so nervous that he could hardly speak to his bride, but when he called to the fox there was no reply.

Meanwhile the fox had run far ahead of the caravan and had come face to face with a team of traders travelling with thirty camels. The fox ran up to them with fear in his eyes and pointed down the road in the direction of the caravan.

'A gang of thieves is coming down this road and unless you turn back now you will be killed!' cried the fox.

The traders gazed into the distance and saw the dust disturbed by the horses' hooves billowing in the air. They knew it was too late to escape and so they turned to the fox for help.

'There is only one way you can escape with your lives,' advised the fox. 'When they pass by you must bow and say that you are under the command of Emperor Mu Tai.'

To Mu Tai's amazement the traders bowed low in homage as his caravan passed by.

By now the fox had met a team of herders and their horses farther down the road and in the same frightened voice he repeated the story of the thieves. The herders also saw the clouds of dust as the caravan approached and they too begged the fox for help.

'I think you will escape with your lives if you bow in

front of the thieves and say that you are Emperor Mu Tai's grooms!'

The herders did as they had been told and the princess was impressed at the loyalty of her husband's citizens. To Mu Tai's amazement he received the same respect from everyone he passed – farmers, merchants and beggars.

The fox was nearly exhausted from a day's running when he spotted a devil's palace carved into a mountainside near Mu Tai's home. He slipped past the guards and made his way to the devil's bedroom. The devil was just falling asleep when the fox leaped onto his bed and pulled him to the floor.

'Your Majesty, save yourself!' cried the fox in despair. 'As I speak, hundreds of thieves are attacking the walls of your palace. They have vowed to kill you. You must hide over here in the space behind your stove.'

While the devil squeezed himself into the small hiding-place behind the stove, the fox piled logs on the fire. It burned so fiercely that the devil pleaded for mercy. The fox continued to feed the roaring fire so that the devil fainted and was slowly roasted alive. Then the ingenious fox threw the devil's ashes out of the window and strutted through the palace announcing the death of the devil Emperor and the arrival of a new ruler.

The palace servants lined the rooms to greet the new couple. Mu Tai became the new Emperor and appointed the fox his chief minister. After months of wise and sympathetic government Mu Tai and his wife grew to be loved by their servants and they ruled peacefully for many years. But before the Emperor made any decisions he consulted the fox, who never failed to produce clever counsel.

After ten years in the palace the fox died and Mu Tai declared that his dearest friend should always be remembered. He made the fox's golden fur into a hat and the people throughout Hsin Chiang liked it so much that whenever a fox died they did the same. That is why to this day the people of Hsin Chiang are famous for their fox-fur hats.

Pai Hua Lake

A broad river flows through the bustling city of Szechuan.
It is said that during the T'ang dynasty its banks were
crowded with shops and houses and every day the unmarried girls of the town went down to the water to wash
their clothes.

One afternoon a man came running down to the river
urging the girls to come and see a strange monk who had
just arrived in the town. The girls hurriedly finished beating their clothes against the rocks and packed them in
straw baskets, anxious to see the unusual stranger. Only
one girl remained by the river. No amount of persuasion
would convince Jung Ch'ing to leave her washing until it
was properly done.

Her companions made their way towards the town but
stopped short as they saw the figure of the strange monk
walking towards them. The girls drew back in horror as
he silently made his way down to the river, ignoring the
whispers and muttered exclamations. They cringed at the
sight of his scarred, wrinkled face, his ulcerated feet and
his torn, sun-bleached robe. He knelt down at the water's

edge and cupped his hands together to drink from the river. Everybody, except Jung Ch'ing, moved back to avoid the stench from his body. When he asked for food they turned their backs, but Jung Ch'ing offered him the hospitality of her home. Her friends tried to persuade her not to go near the monk, but she pushed her way through the crowds and led him down the dark, narrow streets of the town.

Jung Ch'ing cooked a simple meal of beans and rice which the monk devoured eagerly without thanking her. No sooner had he finished eating than he demanded a bed and, without hesitation, Jung Ch'ing offered him hers. In the morning the monk asked to be fed again and she offered him her remaining rice. While he ate quietly she went to the bedroom and removed the bedsheet which was covered in blood and dirt from the monk's body. As she folded it into her washing basket the monk asked if she could also wash his robes. Jung Ch'ing did not have the heart to refuse. When she picked up his robe, flakes of dry skin fell on her dress and fleas leaped into her face and hair, but she realized that she only had to hold the robe for a minute but the monk had to wear it all the time.

On their way to the river the other washing girls kept their distance from Jung Ch'ing and the monk, but out of curiosity they followed the couple down to the water's edge. When Jung Ch'ing had lowered the robe into the water it mysteriously changed to a brilliant white. The crowd closed in to see what power or magic the robe contained. Jung Ch'ing rubbed the white cloth between her hands and a lotus flower appeared on the water. She rubbed the cloth again and another lotus flower appeared. While the crowd watched in stunned amazement she continued to rub the cloth until there was a long trail of lotus blossoms floating down to the Pai Hua lake at the end of the river.

'It's a priceless magic robe,' cried one of the girls as she ran towards the water to touch it. But before she could reach it the robe flew out of Jung Ch'ing hands and landed at the monk's feet. He bent down, lifted the robe and wrapped it around his body, and as it touched his skin all his sores and ulcers disappeared.

A golden light now radiated from the monk's body and he smiled in gratitude at Jung Ch'ing as he was lifted to Heaven by the wind. When the washing girls caught their last glimpse of the monk he was standing on a white cloud and they realized that they had mocked an Immortal in disguise.

Jung Ch'ing had been rewarded by the blessings of the Immortals and not long after she met and married a man who was honest and wise. When news of her good fortune spread, this part of the river became a popular place in which to marry. To this day the river is known as the Washing River and the Pai Hua lake overflows with lotus flowers. Each year, on the 19th day of the 4th month, hundreds of people come to the lake to sail on decorated boats during the Huan Flower Ceremony in memory of Jung Ch'ing and the Immortal.

The Islands of the Immortals

Many thousands of years ago the Immortals lived happily and peacefully on five islands which floated on the Eastern Sea. They drank the morning dew, feasted on heavenly fruits and lived in palaces of jade. Free from work and worries, the Immortals passed their time visiting each other or travelling across the sky on clouds.

The only time the Immortals argued with one another was when their idyllic existence was interrupted by storms. When the sea was hit by squalls or struck by hurricanes, the islands were tossed in the water. The Immortals had to fly to Heaven for safety and wait until the storm had passed. It usually took them several days to recover after one of these disasters and even longer to find the islands, which had been scattered across the Eastern Sea.

One evening, after a particularly severe hurricane, the Immortals petitioned the Jade Emperor to persuade the Sea God to secure their islands to the sea bed. When the Sea God received his orders from the Jade Emperor he swam the length and breadth of the Eastern Sea looking for creatures who were capable of this job. It was a fruitless

search but when he returned to his palace he was inspired
by the sight of the tortoise guard and ordered them to tie
the islands to their backs. Once the tortoises were in place
and the islands were secured to their hard shells nothing
could uproot them and the Immortals were content.

After several years of peace the Immortals noticed that
their islands were subject to earth tremors and once again
they petitioned the Jade Emperor for help. When the Jade
Emperor asked the Sea God for an explanation he was
told that the tortoises were bored after sitting still for so
long and needed to take some exercise. The Sea God hit
upon a solution and asked the tortoises to move to a new
island once a year. The tortoises agreed and the immortals
were left in relative peace for three thousand years.

A race of giants known as the Lung Po Kuo lived on
the far side of the easternmost island. When they stood
up their heads brushed the clouds and when they walked
their footprints left deep hollows in the land. One of their
footsteps was equal to the number of steps a human would
make in a lifetime.

The giants had always lived peacefully with the immortals and with Heaven but one day a young giant disrupted
the harmony of the islands. He decided to spend a day
fishing and perched himself on the rocks above the water
so he could have a clear view of the sea bed. During the
morning the sea was empty, but in the afternoon the giant
caught sight of the tortoises taking their annual exercise.
He loaded his line with bait and as the greedy tortoises
fought to eat the lumps of fresh fish on his line the islands
floated out to sea. No sooner had the giant hauled one
tortoise onto the shore than the next tortoise would appear
on the surface waiting for the bait. Within an hour the
giant had caught all five tortoises and had tied them upside
down on his carrying pole.

That night the islands were struck by a severe hurricane
that ripped them from the water and sent them tumbling
across the ocean. Two were carried by the winds to the

North Pole and sank to the bottom of the ocean and the other three were flung to the most distant corner of the Eastern Sea. The Immortals were furious at the giant's carelessness and took refuge in the clouds until the hurricane had subsided. When the winds ceased, their islands could no longer be seen. They flew to the Jade Emperor to complain. As punishment for the giant's carelessness the Jade Emperor summoned his most powerful magic and shrank every giant of the Lung Po Kuo nation. One moment the giants could touch the clouds and the next they were no higher than a pine tree and that is how they remained for eternity.

Meanwhile the Sea God had managed to retrieve three of the islands and ordered three more tortoises to support them but they were forbidden ever to move again. Once more everything was peaceful in the Eastern Sea but the immortals refused to return to their homes. They packed their bags and scattered across Heaven and earth where they found more restful places.

The three islands in the Eastern Sea have not moved since that fateful hurricane. Sailors who have been lost in uncharted waters have reported seeing three mysterious mountains rising through the morning mists, but they have never managed to reach them.

Into the Lion's Mouth

Wang Chung and his younger brother Wang Hsaio lived in a small town in southern China. They had never been good friends but had been forced to make a joint living on a small plot of land bequeathed to them by their dead parents. Wang Hsaio was as generous as his brother was selfish and, as fate would have it, Wang Chung married a woman equally heartless and unkind. The new wife loathed her brother-in-law and waited for the opportunity to throw him out of her home. One day, exhausted from working in the fields, Wang Hsaio broke a teacup and his sister-in-law used this as an excuse to tell him to leave. As a parting present Wang Chung gave his brother a wooden hoe and a thin straw mattress.

Clutching his two worldly possessions, Wang Hsaio walked for several days through villages and towns he had heard of but never seen before. On the fifth night he came across a desolate, uninhabited strip of land. At the centre lay a ruined temple, its once polished floors overgrown with weeds. Desperate for a place to spend the night he headed towards the temple. The walls were crumbling and the sky was visible through the rotten roof, but a finely carved lion stood in the courtyard as clean and elegant as the day it had been erected. Considering this a good omen, Wang Hsaio decided to make this his temporary home.

With a small amount of money borrowed from a local moneylender, he bought enough grain to farm the land around the temple and, while waiting for his crops to grow, he trapped animals and picked wild fruit. He spent his days working and his evenings sitting alone on the temple doorstep; nobody came to visit him and he avoided the people of the village. The stone lion guarding the temple seemed to be his only friend and in his loneliness he struck up a one-sided friendship with the lion. He built the creature a reed shelter and gave him offerings each morning. Every evening he held long conversations with the lion, who sat still and proud but nevertheless seemed to be listening.

One humid summer's evening Wang Hsaio sat as usual discussing his crops with the lion while fanning his face with a fan.

'My stone lion, you don't know how lucky you are. You can sit here all day without a worry in the world while I exhaust myself in the fields. Even now, after all these weeks of work, I still don't know if my crops will give a good harvest.'

As usual the lion listened but Wang Hsaio said nothing more – he just sat at the lion's feet, lost in thought. Almost imperceptibly the ground began to shake and what began as a slight shudder soon grew into a rumble. Afraid that a storm was breaking, Wang Hsaio crept into the lion's shelter and huddled against his cold body.

'Don't worry, I'll protect you,' said a deep voice above his head.

'How can you speak? You're made of stone!' cried Wang Hsaio in disbelief.

'I have told you, don't worry and don't ask questions.

189

Put your hand into my mouth and take whatever you find there,' ordered the lion.

Wang Hsaio did as he had been told and pulled out a nugget of silver. He thanked the lion profusely.

'Don't thank me yet,' roared his friend. 'There's plenty more in my mouth. Help yourself, take as much as you want.'

Wang Hsaio reached again into the stone mouth and hauled out a handful of gold and silver. He put it carefully into a hessian sack that lay at his feet. The lion kept his mouth open so Wang Hsaio could take even more money, but the boy was satisfied with what he had.

Wang Hsaio wanted to share his good fortune with his brother and set off on the long journey home. When he reached his brother's house he was so excited he rushed in without knocking and emptied the bag of gold and silver coins onto the floor. No sooner had he related the story of the stone lion than his brother grabbed him roughly by the collar and demanded to know the whereabouts of the temple. Wang Hsaio had barely finished speaking when Wang Chung ran out of the door and disappeared into the dark winding streets.

He passed through unfamiliar villages and towns as his brother had done before him and on the fifth night he reached the temple clearing. Greedy for riches, he ran into the courtyard. 'Open your mouth, open your mouth!' he screamed at the stone lion. But the lion remained impassive.

Wang Chung picked up a small boulder that lay beside the temple wall and hurled it at the lion's mouth. The lion roared in pain as the boulder struck the side of his face and as he opened his mouth Wang Chung stuck his arm deep inside. He wrenched the money out before the lion had time to close his jaws.

As Wang Chung was securing the top of his first sack of money, the lion finally had a chance to speak.

'You've taken enough,' he growled. 'I can't keep my

mouth open for ever and you have enough money to last you a lifetime.'

But before the stone lion could close his mouth Wang Chung had once more stuck his arm inside. This time the lion's teeth shut tight on his arm and no matter how hard he pulled and struggled the lion refused to loosen his grip. Wang Chung screamed and shouted for help but his cries were lost in the howling wind which had suddenly arisen. Soon the sky was darkened by rain clouds and every few minutes the temple courtyard was illuminated by streaks of lightning. When the storm finally broke, the rain fell with such force that it streamed from the broken gutters of the temple and formed small rivers through the earth. As Wang Chung clutched his bag of money with his free hand and fought to prise the other from the lion's jaws, to his horror he saw the sack dwindle in size as it became soaked in water. Like acid the rain was slowly dissolving the gold and silver and it was being washed away in the rivulets of water that swirled around him.

The storm passed and the night closed in, but the lion showed no sign of tiring. One week passed before Wang Chung's wife found her husband collapsed in exhaustion against the lion's body, his hand firmly trapped in its mouth. The stone lion listened impassively as Wang Chung told his wife how he had found and lost the money, but before she had even heard the full story she picked up a stone from the floor and hurled it at his captor's head. The stone broke into small fragments when it hit the lion's head but the animal did not flinch.

'Don't do that!' cried Wang Chung. 'You will only make him more determined to keep me imprisoned here. If he wanted, he could crush my bones to powder between his teeth, so we must wait until he is ready. Go and find Wang Hsaio. He might be able to persuade the lion to open his mouth.'

Wang Chung's wife sullenly agreed to her husband's plea and returned home to find her brother-in-law. She

scoured the town but he had already left with his newfound
fortune. She knew no one else who had the power to free
her husband and so, for the next three months, she rented
a room in a nearby village and made a daily journey to the
temple to feed him. By the end of that time their savings
had run out and all she could offer her husband was a
stale rice bun.

Wang Chung was now so weak and thin that he barely
had the strength to eat. His wife fed him like a child and
then, as she ate what was left over, she began to cry. She
was suddenly brought to her senses by a deep laugh that
came from the lion's mouth, and as he laughed Wang
Chung's trapped arm was freed.

'You've learned your lesson,' roared the lion. 'I promise
that if you take care of me, I will take care of you.'

From that day the couple took over their brother's abandoned farmland around the temple. They tidied the temple
courtyard, they cared for the grounds, they made offerings
before the shrine, and each day they laid flowers at the
lion's feet. The lion never spoke again, but in return for
their care he made sure that their land was always fruitful.